Maurice Walsh,
Storyteller

1934 Portrait by Sean O'Sullivan, R.H.A.

MAURICE WALSH, STORYTELLER

STEVE MATHESON

BRANDON

First Published 1985
Brandon Book Publishers Ltd.
Dingle, Co. Kerry, Ireland;
and 51 Washington Street, Dover,
New Hampshire 03820, U.S.A.

ISBN 0 86322 052 5 hardback

ISBN 0 86322 062 2 paperback

The author wishes to thank Maurice Walsh and the *Irish Press* for permission
to reproduce the photographs which appear in this book.

This book is published with the financial assistance of the Arts Council/An
Chomhairle Ealaíon, Ireland.

Jacket and cover design: Syd Bluett

Typesetting: Setleaders Ltd., Phototypesetting, Dublin, Ireland.

Printed by: Billings Ltd.

Author's Acknowledgements

It is my pleasure to acknowledge the extensive help, kindness and encouragement I have received in writing this biography. Many people in Ireland, particularly in Kerry, and in the north-east of Scotland gave unstintingly of assistance and if I do not mention them all by name it is due more to lack of space than of inclination. All those I was able to contact who had known Maurice Walsh gave generously of their time and their memories. They recognised, I think, that what I was hoping to produce was an affectionate tribute to a writer who gave much pleasure and a man who generated much kindness.

I am grateful to Messrs W & R Chambers Ltd for permission to quote from Maurice's books and from his introduction to *Scotch Whisky: A Guide* by J. Marshall Robb; to the Curtis Publishing Co for permission to quote from the *Saturday Evening Post* article "Ireland in a Warring Europe"; to the Irish Excise Officer's Association for permission to quote from their journal and yearbook. I have been unable to contact those now responsible for defunct journals like the *Shannonside Annual* and the *Irish Emerald* but acknowledge the sources where they are used.

My warm thanks go to Mr Bryan MacMahon, Mr John B. Keane and his wife Mary and Mr Michael Kennelly in Listowel, Kerry, and to Mrs Betty Fleming in Keith, Banffshire, Scotland. Mr Andrew Melvin of Tain, Rosshire, Scotland was a source of great encouragement and I am grateful to him for that and for sight of and permission to quote from so many letters from Maurice to Andrew's late wife, Dorothy, Maurice's niece. I am indebted, too, to Mr Seamus Paircir of the Irish Revenue for making available much information about Maurice's early career and about his involvement with the excise association, Comhaltas Cana.

My special thanks, gratitude and continuing affection go to the Walsh family, for access to and permission to quote from the Walsh papers, for a wealth of anecdote and for the finest possible help and encouragement. I must mention especially Maurice's three sons, Maurice, Ian and Neil, and his grandson, Maurice. They and their families made this book possible. They provided what is best in it. The faults and inaccuracies are my own.

Perhaps the most telling commentary on a man lies in the personalities of his sons. Maurice Walsh had three whose warmth and charm made research for this book not only possible but immensely pleasant and rewarding. Ian, alas, is no longer with us but through his own generous, effervescent nature there shone the very image of his father's appeal. He, too, was a small man, with a twinkling eye, a golden tongue and a heart big enough to encompass the whole world. Maurice and Neil have the same warmth and deep humour and such an abiding sense of the need for a man to be true to the ideals of decency and honour that their code (and through them their father's code) is tangible to the observer. Maurice's grandson, Maurice, who lived with him from childhood, is of the same breed. All four made Maurice Walsh live again for me, in laughter and sometimes near to tears.

Contents

To my sons

Introduction: 21 April 1879.

Monday, 21 April 1879, was not a particularly eventful day in the history of the British Empire, nor yet in that part of the realm called Ireland. No major battles were fought, although the Zulu War was rumbling on and there had been yet another disaster for the British army, at Isandula. According to *The Kerry Sentinel*, the War Department was about to adopt war balloons for land and sea use and it was proposed to send a few to Zululand. *The Irish Times* began its editorial that day: "The student of British history will have to scan his annals very closely for a period when the nation was more curiously engaged in a variety of small troubles than it is just now."

Yet the troubles were not so small and difficult times lay ahead. Years of agrarian turmoil were by no means over and that very year Michael Davitt was planning the Mayo Land League in pursuit of the idea of restoring the land to the Irish. Gladstone's reforms had not borne fruit. On the mainland he had announced his decision not to stand for Greenwich at the next election and was soon to begin the historic Midlothian campaign. A demonstration in his favour had taken place the previous Saturday at Bonnyrigg in Midlothian, where fireclay workers carried banners emblazoned with the words: "Gladstone is a brick and on him we build our hopes."

In Ireland the omens were not hopeful. Money was scarce and there had been seven lean years after the collapse of the Egyptian trade. Sailings to America continued to cream off the young and the adventurous. Steamships of the State Line sailed weekly from Glasgow, calling at Larne. The ship *State of Nevada* was due to leave on 26 April and the steerage fare was six guineas. Those who preferred Canada could get to Quebec from Liverpool on the Dominion Line, also for six guineas steerage. America was the promised land, full of easy money it seemed. A lady called Van Berg had just won a thousand dollars after walking 372 miles in the Women's Walking Match at Gilmore's in New York. *The Irish Times* thought that was degrading.

Closer to home, the South of Ireland Temperance League was holding a Congress at Waterford to support the Saturday Closing Bill. At the Killultagh Hunt Steeplechase on that Monday, 21 April, the favourites in all five races went down and the bookmakers were smiling. At the Tralee Petty Sessions, there were over one hundred cases on the book for hearing that day, of which sixty-one were brought at the suit of the Constabulary. John Cluse of Boherbee was summoned for having his licenced premises open at an illegal time (fifteen minutes past nine o'clock on Good Friday). The Chairman of the Bench, Sir Henry Donovan, declined to accept the assertion of Head Constable Patrick Murtagh that although the two men he had found on the premises had been glassless, the assumption was that they had been drinking. Sir Henry made it clear that he knew the defendant and the premises well and had no hesitation in accepting that drink would not have been sold. The worthy Mr Cluse was fined ten shillings for being open but the offence was not to be recorded on his licence.

In another case James and John Walsh of Ballysheen were charged with assault on Patrick Trant and Maurice Moriarty. In a confused welter of cross charges it was difficult to decide who had assaulted whom but John Walsh got a week in gaol.

In a different part of Kerry that day a significant event occured for another Walsh family. At Ballydonoghue, between Listowel and Ballybunion, Maurice Walsh, the·third child and first son of John and Elizabeth Buckley Walsh, was born.

Part 1.

Mashing.

The Early Years: 1879 - 1901.

Chapter 1. **Ballydonoghue and Family History.**

Ballydonoghue is a small farming community between Listowel and the seaside resort of Ballybunion in North Kerry. It is a comfortable, relaxed countryside, more prosperous today than it was a hundred years ago but with the same slow, contented air. The old style, long narrow farmhouses, with their thatched roofs, pumps in the yard and common interior layouts of women's room, kitchen, "the room" for visitors, men's room and loft, have nearly all fallen into decay and been replaced by bright new bungalows. O'Sullivan's bar is still there, though, with its neatly thatched roof and cool dark room where the turf fire is said never to have gone out this century. Its combined bar and shop were and are the natural centre for the little community and it has, therefore, survived intact when the old farmhouses no longer meet the needs of their people.

Yet if the buildings have changed the lie of the enduring land remains the same, "from Pubil Dotha to Trienafludig, from Galey Cross to Cnucanor".[1] This calm, peaceful valley beneath the gentle swell of Cnucanor sits on the edge of some of the most enchantingly beautiful country in the world but it has its own charm and Maurice Walsh never tired of describing it.

From the heathery head of Cnucanor you get one of the finest, widest views in all Ireland. On one hand you look over Clare to Galway Bay and on the other to the Paps of Killarney above the high shoulder of Slieve Mish; eastwards, the hills of Barragh hedge the plains of North Desmond; westwards and ever westwards is the lifting plain of the Atlantic sea, and if your sight is good enough and light — as the scientists tell us — is curved, you can see the skyscrapers of New York; and below you is the Vale of Tralee, verdant in woods and pastures shining with running waters.[2]

Ballydonoghue itself is passed in a car before you know it is there, on the straight road that runs through from Listowel to Lisselton Cross and on to Ballybunion. There is nothing to prompt idle travellers to stop, unless they fancy a drink in O'Sullivan's and find themselves soon in the middle of a good crack which justifies the stop in itself. They remember Maurice Walsh well there. However, there is little to call attention to the history of the area, although history in plenty is there for the knowing. Cnucanor itself — Cnoc an Áir, the hill of slaughter — takes its name from one of the gory battles of the Fianna. Or perhaps, according to another interpretation, it is Cnoc an Óir, the hill of gold – fairy gold at that. Slaughter seems to have the edge, though. And there was bloodshed there in more recent times too.

Nearly thirty years before Maurice Walsh was born at Ballydonoghue, the man who was to find fame as Lord Kitchener was born in 1850 at Crotter House, a Georgian mansion in the parish, four miles to the north-west of Listowel, although there is little to commemorate that event either. Kitchener's contempt for the Irish is well known and was exceeded only by their disdain of him. No one mentions him in North Kerry today but there are still some interesting local stories about his father's schemes for improving the return on farming investment by introducing new ideas. One was to feed pigs free in the woods instead of keeping them locked up in sties and bringing food expensively to them. The Irish pigs of those days were notably long in the leg and when released took off joyously like greyhounds to root madly in every farm around, at considerable later cost in compensation and embarrassment. Then there was an attempt to fatten up goats for market, an impossible task since goats are all belly.

The Walshes had been in that part of North Kerry for generations, certainly back to the sixteenth century when one of them was hanged, probably for wrecking. They were seafarers as well as farmers. The area has a long history of violence, agrarian troubles, rebellion and strife in which Walshes appear from time to time. They got into scrapes and intrigues abroad too. One James Walsh was captain of the ship which took James II to France when he fled the country. Unable to return, the captain set up a shipbuilding firm in Nantes. His son Francis prospered in merchanting and Francis' son Anthony provided the frigate which took Bonnie Prince Charlie to Scotland in 1745, *La Doutelle*. He was said to be a small man with a beaked nose and he was ennobled by Louis XV as Antoine de Walsh, Comte de Serrant. On the mantelpiece of the library at the Chateau de Serrant at St George-sur-Loire is a painting of Prince Charles Edward Stuart giving instructions to Antoine de Walsh to take back to the court of France. A later Walsh entombed in the chateau chapel is described as Theobald de Walsh de Dublin. The coat of arms above the chateau gate is a swan transfixed by an arrow with the motto "Transfixus sed non mortuus". Maurice Walsh the author "translated" it in his own inimitable style as, "We always went to the fight and we always fell." The last Walsh at Serrant, Valentine, married into the de Tremouille family and the chateau has remained in that family's hands ever since.

Another seafaring Walsh, John, who was born in Dublin on 7 June 1743 and died in Philadelphia on 24 April 1828, was a captain in the Continental navy with letters of marque and reprisal and was a cousin to Thomas Fitzsimmons, one of the signers of the Constitution. Maurice Walsh himself claimed kinship with both these branches of the Walsh family and adopted the motto "Transfixus sed non mortuus" as his own.[3]

In Ireland itself the Walshes were not strangers to violent action, though even then enlivened by typically wry Walsh humour. This is best illustrated by the Walsh involvement in the faction fight at Ballyeagh strand on 24 June 1834. Faction fighting was a peculiarly Irish nineteenth century phenomenon which was at least passively encouraged by the authorities as a useful way of ensuring that the native Irish dissipated their violent (and potentially rebellious) energies against each other. Factions were groups of families and friends, often numbering hundreds, who fought other factions with fists, sticks and stones, either as a result of some real or imagined insult or for the sheer hell of it. The fight at Ballyeagh strand on the Cashen estuary in North Kerry was one of the bloodiest. A huge force of the faction known as Lawlor – Black Mulvihills (their enemies called them Bald Mulvihills) met and eventually defeated the faction known as the Cooleens in a battle which left some twenty dead and hundreds wounded. One of the wounded was Maurice Walsh's great grandfather Tom, who made his way back to Ballydonoghue early in the fight with blood streaming from a head wound and soaking his shirt. The Walshes were related to the Mulvihills by marriage and this Walsh was wild with pain and dismay that the Cooleens appeared to be winning.

"Give us a clean shirt," he begged his wife as she tended his wound, "and let me drown meself for there's divil the hope."

That calm woman replied easily, "Sure, if ye are goin' to drown yourself, wouldn't the shirt ye have on do just as well?" But he did not drown himself and after a late rally the Mulvihills won the fight.

This man's son Maurice Walsh married particularly well, to one of the Lyons of North Kerry – a "match". He had two farms close together, one at Ballydonoghue of about one hundred acres and the other at Gunnsborough. Ballydonoghue went to his son John and Gunnsborough to John's younger brother Paddy. John was a small man in the Lyons tradition. In time there was a third place at Gloura. Paddy was a grand farmer and saw to the running of all three farms with great energy.

John Walsh of Ballydonoghue was from all accounts a remarkable man. He had a passion for books and stayed happily at school and college until he was twenty-two. There was a vague intention that he should be an accountant or a butter buyer, a very lucrative career in those days, the late 1860s and early 1870s. However, he was only really interested in books and horses. When his sister Ellen died of tuberculosis in 1872 his parents brought him home to the farm in a panic and there he stayed.

One very practical thing John had learned was how to survey using a chain, which he did free of charge for all his neighbours for miles around. Everyone knew him and he was widely acknowledged as a very clever man. His reputation and authority, which grew over the years, were eventually put to the test in 1900. An American visiting Ballybunion managed to cause more than usual irritation by airing his profound knowledge at length about every conceivable subject. The hotel keeper William O'Sullivan, a canny man not given to hasty action, reached the point where he could stand the strain no longer and bet the American five pounds, a huge sum in those days, that he could find a man to better him in discussion before that evening was out. The American was a sporting man and readily agreed, so the doughty William sent for John Walsh.

Word of the bet spread like wildfire and by the time the pony and trap returned with John the street in front of the hotel was black with people eager to witness the contest, and in the hotel itself it was barely possible to lift a glass. William O'Sullivan was doing grand business however the contest went. At length the two men settled on the veranda of the hotel where the maximum number of people could hear them and talk began, helped on its way with pints of porter and the enthusiastic comments of the crowd. The two men spoke at length about history, geography, horses and literature and in the end there was no doubt that victory on points lay with John Walsh. The American paid up handsomely and the whole five pounds was spent on free drinks in the hotel that night.

John himself did a little about the farm but always had a hired man. The most famous of these was Paddy Bawn Enright, whose name John's son Maurice was to immortalise in the most famous of all his stories, "The Quiet Man". John Walsh let it be known that he was looking for a lad about the place and Paddy Bawn's mother sent him along one morning when John Walsh was sitting at his breakfast in the kitchen. John looked up as the nervous seventeen year old poked his head in over the half door.

"Who are you, boy?"

"I'm Paddy Bawn, sir. I've come to work for you."

"You have, eh. Well, you'll do, boy. Sit in to your breakfast now."

And Paddy Bawn stayed till he died. He was a very dark lad with jet black hair so it was inevitable that he should be called Paddy Bawn – White Patrick. He was soon one of the family and a great friend to John Walsh and to his sons. In later years, when the old man could no longer walk to mass, Paddy Bawn took him to the chapel in a donkey cart and carried him up to the gallery. Those were the days when landowners and their families sat apart in the gallery. At the last Gospel, when normally all stand, only those in the gallery stood, John Walsh among them with Paddy Bawn as one of the family to lend him a strong arm and keep him on his feet. When John was dying in 1936 at the age of eighty-six, Paddy Bawn sat up with him along with John's youngest daughter Julia every night for a fortnight, talking quietly to the old man about the doings of their neighbours and the little events of the day. When the night was over and the daylight brought John some ease, Paddy went out to keep the work of the farm going. The relationship was master and man, with affection and understanding on both sides.

When "The Quiet Man" originally appeared in the *Saturday Evening Post* in 1933, Maurice Walsh used the name "Sean Kelvin". By the time it appeared in the book *Green Rushes* in 1935, he had changed the name to Paddy Bawn Enright. The character in the book bears little resemblance to the real life Paddy Bawn other than in his steadfastness, but using the name was a tribute from Maurice Walsh to a lifelong friend. It was a gesture he used often, but never so effectively as with "The Quiet Man". After the film appeared in 1952 Paddy Bawn became a local legend and revelled in it. He was not the explosive Tiger Enright of the story, but didn't he fight a bit in his youth when he had drink taken? He did, but sure there was never any harm in him.

John Walsh himself liked to spend his time reading, drinking pints of porter and going to the races. He was an authority on blood horses, as was his father Maurice. His parents lived with him at Ballydonoghue until, at the age of twenty-five, he married Elizabeth Buckley from Tollemar, near Listowel. Then they went to Paddy at Gunnsborough.

Racing was a passion with John Walsh, whether it was "leppers" or just straight flat racing. He went to every meeting he could, in spite of his wife's strong disapproval. He and his friends thought nothing of walking twenty or thirty miles to a meeting and back, keeping themselves going with frequent nips of whiskey. Elizabeth Buckley was a strong minded lady and her disapproval covered the whiskey as well as the racing, but she could not move John. Curiously enough, though, after she died, on 29 December 1913, he never went to another race meeting as a public mark of respect and of love for her. He never missed a bet on the Grand National, though.

Elizabeth Buckley's people originally came from Cork where one of her forebears had been Lord Mayor. Her grandfather had six sons and he acquired six farms in Kerry for them, as well as six Kerry wives. John and Elizabeth had ten children, two of whom died young. First there were two daughters, Ellie May, who was born in

1875 but died in infancy, and Bridget (Bridgie) in 1877. The first son, Maurice, was born in 1879 on 21 April, though his *Who's Who* entry says 2 May. (He enjoyed that and claimed two birthdays, but his wife allowed him only one each year!) After Maurice came Timothy (1881), Hannie (1883) who became a nun and was known as Sister Gabriel, Mary (1885), Paddy (1887), Lily (1888) who died of croup at the age of three, Mick (1889) and Julia (1892).

Chapter 2. **Boyhood and Youth**

At the time Maurice Walsh was born there were five other families in the Ballydonoghue area: Kings, O'Connells, Crimminses, O'Sullivans and Buckleys. When Maurice was a youngster there were fifty-four children between the six families. He had a happy and healthy childhood and it coloured his whole life.

> "We were all great singers in our place, except my father. He could not sing a note – only, maybe, the morning of a races, but he was a very knowledgeable man all the same. He knew all about horses, racehorses."
>
> "One of the evils of Ireland, I believe?"
>
> "'Tis so, ma'am – same as good whiskey and pretty women. My father says the Lamb was the best horse ever looked through a bridle. A black horse, with grey points, fifteen-two and he won the National twice."[4]

That was one of Maurice Walsh's characters, Paddy Joe Long in his second book *While Rivers Run*, published in 1928 when Maurice's father was still alive, but it is John Walsh he is talking about there, as it is when he says:

> My father was very fond of coffee, but he used to drink it to keep himself awake. He went in for a debauch of coffee and Dickens at the same time. He had a great pile of tattered blue covered volumes of *All the Year Round*, and when my mother would see him of a night haul a bundle out of their press she used never say a word but brew him a big pot of coffee. She made it in a brown earthenware pot, same as you'd make tea, and drew it over the greesoch – red hot peat embers ... It would lift the top of your head off. My father used read half the night, drinking cups of it and smoking like a kiln. I mind the first book I read, I read over his shoulder. It was a story by Robert Buchanan called *Matt: A Tale of a Caravan* – about a wandering artist and a Welsh maid. My father was a faster reader than I was, but he always waited at the end of the page for me. That's the kind of man he was. It was my first glimpse into romance, and never again in heaven or in hell will I get a glimpse like it.[5]

That is pure autobiography. The only detail omitted from real life was the way in which Maurice's mother used to bring these sessions to an end. There they would be, father and son reading slowly and happily by candlelight as the night wore on. When Elizabeth decided that it was time for Maurice to go to bed, she took action quietly, so as not to disturb the other children. An accurately thrown cork would hit John or maybe Maurice on the nose or cheek and when they looked up, there would be Elizabeth at the door. She was adamant, and bed it then had to be.

Maurice Walsh all his life acknowledged the deep debt he owed both his parents, but his father in particular. His *Who's Who* entry describes him as "son of John Walsh, farmer and Land Leaguer". That short phrase speaks volumes. Maurice admired his father immensely, though he did not always agree with him on every count. John Walsh was a pro-Britisher and did not want de Valera, while Maurice did. In *The Road To Nowhere* which appeared in 1934 Maurice made a gentle reference to the argument when he has one of his characters say that his "friend, John Walsh of Ballydonoghue, hasn't slep' a night since de Valera won the election". By that time, Maurice was having his own differences with Dev's government, but that is a later story.

John Walsh had a fine library of the classics – Scott, Dickens, Thackeray and the like – and was extremely well read, up to and including Conan Doyle. But his proudest moment was seeing a whole window in Eason's bookshop in Dublin devoted to a display of his son's books.

From his very earliest years, Maurice was accustomed to listen to stories from his father and his father's friends. John Walsh was steeped in legend and folk tales which were hard and real for him and became so for his son. Years later some of these found their way into Maurice's books, stories like the beautiful and lyrical tale of the Colleen Oge in *Green Rushes* which was closely based on the experiences of Ellen Molouney, whose sister worked for a time on the Walsh farm; or like the moving tale "My Fey Lady" of the chapel on Christmas Eve nearly empty of folk but filled with a growing press and stifling atmosphere of a great but unseen congregation. It was from his father too that Maurice got the first intimation of the theory of place that was to run through so many of his books and which is clearly articulated in "My Fey Lady".

A place acquires an entity of its own, an entity that is the essence of all the life and thoughts and griefs and joys that have gone before; and it might be that it was the soul of the place that was in tune with a girl sib to itself.[6]

This is not to suggest that John Walsh was fey but he certainly passed on to his son Maurice something of his own awareness of the uncanny in life as well as of the marvellous in literature.

Maurice himself was bright and lively as a child, naturally inquisitive and eager for new experiences and challenges. It was a trait to stay with him all his life. Once, when he was six years old, he came home a bit later than usual from school at Lisselton, a mile or so up the road. He often was late from playing with the other children on the way home but this time he refused to eat and went to sleep in the little chair set for him near his father's seat by the fire. His mother picked him up and put him to bed without thinking too much about it but when she could not waken him in the morning she sent John off in a panic to fetch the doctor from Listowel. Dr O'Connell did manage to rouse the boy in the end and diagnosed simple exhaustion. John got the full story when he met the schoolmaster Master Dillon next day and found out that Maurice had not been to school at all but had walked the four miles to Ballybunion after hearing some of the older boys talking about going off to the seashore, spent the whole day roaming around the coast and then walked all the way back home again.

School at Lisselton brought a major influence into Maurice's life in the person of his first teacher Michael Dillon, a legendary man in a long tradition of learning at Lisselton going back to Grey Patrick O'Connor in 1745. Master Dillon lived to be one hundred years old and to the end of his days former pupils who had become famous and successful all over the world returned to pay him homage. Maurice Walsh never missed a visit to him whenever he returned to Kerry. Michael was a kindly man who none the less believed in firm discipline and laid down the law both as a teacher and as a father. If a child had a love of learning in him, Michael would coax it out. One of his proudest achievements was to see three brothers in one farming family acknowledged as poets.

The Dillons came from Coolard, a parish nearby, and had been teachers for generations. Michael's son Tom, a famous teacher at Lisselton, made a bilingual Irish and English school there after 1918. He loved the Irish language and gave his life to spreading it through school, evening classes and Saturday classes at the Listowel and Ballybunion convents. He was out afoot in all weathers and died in 1924 when only forty-two. Something of him appears in *The Small Dark Man* when Hugh Forbes describes his own work as a teacher in Kerry. The book appeared in 1929.

A few of us have a notion that Ireland is in a bad way, with wrong ideals out of the mouths of prosperity mongers, and the only remedy, as we see it, is to get hold of the young . . . All we seek is to make them think, and thinking pierces to the bone. 'Tis how I – and better men – are making our clan, gathering and scattering and holding it too; and in good time, it could be, that clan will arise and drive the huckster and the shopkeeper out of Ireland.[7]

That was Tom Dillon. Michael Dillon's other son, also Michael, was a teacher too for a time. He went to America and became a judge. There was one daughter, Nellie, who taught at Lisselton until her retirement and who lived then near the school to which she and her family devoted such loving care for so many years.

John Walsh was often in their house for a chat or to borrow a book from Michael or Tom. Both John and Michael were crazy about detective stories and would seize on a book avidly, even before breakfast if they had put it down unfinished the previous night. Maurice Walsh also developed a taste for detective stories in his later years. He thought that the Americans always wrote the "kickiest" ones.

Michael Dillon started Maurice on the road to learning and it was soon evident that he was bright. His mother was determined that he should become a priest. In those days in Ireland the eldest son, if clever enough, was destined for the priesthood or the Civil Service. Maurice was clever, otherwise he would have had the farm as he wanted. But Church or State it had to be and the farm went to his brother Paddy. Elizabeth Buckley was not to be gainsaid and it was she who stood over the young Maurice while he did his homework and itched to be outside playing with the other boys.

His great friend in those early days was Tom King, who eventually went to America where he died in the early 1960s, not long before Maurice himself. Maurice used his name for the hero of his first novel *The Key Above the Door*, and while much of Maurice himself went into the character, that tale of staunch friendship was also a nostalgic echo of the early days of easy comradeship amongst boys at Ballydonoghue.

If Tom King was the great friend, Jack Brick was the great enemy, yet it is wholly characteristic of Maurice Walsh that he never used that name for any of the villains in his books. Jack Brick was the captain of the Ballybunion football team while Maurice was the captain of the Ballydonoghue team. With fifty-four children in the immediate vicinity of Ballydonoghue, making up a team was no trouble at all. Jack also went to Lisselton school for a time and the two had a memorable fight there in which Maurice was soundly thrashed. Later on they had another shorter set-to on the football field and Maurice again had the worst of it. They met again, though. That third and last fight formed the basis of nearly all the great fights described later in the books. Maurice was in his late teens at the time and in disgrace with his mother after failing the Civil Service examination in Dublin. He had spent all his time in the library reading romances and Irish history, like the *Annals of the Four Masters*, instead of cramming for the exam as he was supposed to. His mother insisted that he come home to prepare for a resit and a friend of John Walsh, a very well known and exceedingly strict old teacher from Ballybunion called Morgan O'Flaherty, offered to take the young man on.

"Send him to me, John," he said, "and I'll beat it into him."

He did, too, until 6.30 every evening.

So there was Maurice, walking four miles to Ballybunion each day and four back. He was fit, perhaps fitter than he had ever been or would be again. He had taken up boxing and was pretty good at it. There was something of a boxing tradition in North Kerry where the career of John L. Sullivan, who though himself born in Boston had parents who came from Kerry, was followed with pride. Every boy in the area with a decent punch or without one saw himself as a future world champion, following in the great John L.'s footsteps.

The third fight with Jack Brick took place while Maurice was working with Morgan O'Flaherty. On his way there one morning he passed a field where a fair number of the Brick clan were working, Jack among them. Remarks were passed about the ineptitude of the Ballydonoghue football team in general and of its captain in particular. When those were ignored, more personal insults followed. Jack himself left off work and hopped menacingly over the low stone wall into Maurice's path. All the Bricks stopped working then to see what would happen. Luckily for Maurice, Tadgh Moriarty, whose sister was to marry Maurice's brother Mick, was passing at the time and stopped to see fair play. Maurice, like many a hero he was to describe in later years, had been beaten twice and was afraid of being beaten the third time. "We always went to the fight and we always fell." But he was more afraid of showing fear and when Jack came at him he took a deep breath, buttoned his jacket and set to. He led with a crushing left hand blow to the body from which poor Jack never recovered. That fight, like the many to follow it in fiction, was determined by the devastatingly weakening effect of solid body blows. Like the villains in the stories, like Red Will Danaher, like Edward Leng and Vivian Stark and the others, Jack Brick could not believe that the little fellow was getting the better of him and he kept taking punishment until he could no longer stand unaided. Maurice had to hold him upright in the end and prop him against the stone wall to stop him from falling over. He went on his way then, whistling, to thunderous applause from the passengers on the Lartigue train, which had stopped as it left the nearby halt at Francis Road on its way to Ballybunion so that everyone could watch the fight. The animosity between Jack and Maurice was well known in the area and they all had an eyeful that day.

The Lartigue is worth a mention here since it was another element in the colourful pattern that made up the North Kerry scene when Maurice Walsh was a young man. Named after Charles Lartigue, its French designer, it was a small but advanced monorail with seats slung either side of the rail, and it ran between Listowel and Ballybunion with a stop at Lisselton Cross and a passing point and halt at Francis Road. It opened in 1888 and closed in 1924. Maurice's brother Michael, who was known as Mick, became the station master—cum porter—cum jack of all trades at Lisselton Cross and retired on pension when it closed in 1924. Maurice said Mick had it all planned from the start so that he could retire at thirty-five. His wife Nellie Moriarty, the sister of the Tadgh Moriarty who was at the Jack Brick fight, was a teacher in Listowel.

From Lisselton Cross on to Ballybunion the train ran in a dead straight line alongside the road and a man with a sparkling pony would wait at Ballydonoghue for a chance to race it against the train along the straight. That always caused tremendous excitement on the train and along the road. Maurice and the other children (and their fathers) would be dancing with enthusiasm. "Come away the train! Come on the pony!" It did not matter a toss which won.

North Kerry was a lively place for an active boy. There was fishing in the Feale and Galey rivers or in the sea if one took a short step to the coast. There was plenty of rough shooting, rabbits and hares, and also ducks and geese. One of the family firearms was a huge Queen Anne duck gun over eight feet long, with which young Maurice once bagged ninety-five curlew with one shot.

The first tinge of sadness came into his life when he was twelve. His little sister Lily died of croup at the age of three after a lingering illness that left his mother haggard and his father distraught. They were a very close family at all times. Nearly seventy years later, Maurice remembered clearly standing at the family grave in Galey churchyard to see her buried.

"That was the first time I knew grief, and I was only twelve. We had an elegant wake and funeral – and sober, for only sixty-four gallons of stout and two gallons of whiskey were needed."[8]

In the following year, 1892, his mother's fond hopes of seeing him a priest one day suffered a set back when a recruiting Franciscan visited the school in search of likely candidates but turned Maurice down. The roguish gleam in his eye gave the Franciscan warning, perhaps, that the Church was not Maurice's vocation.

"I'll not recommend you, boy," he said, "but you'll be a clever man yet." Maurice – Mossie, as he was called – went on from Lisselton to St Michael's College in Listowel to prepare for the Civil Service examination, the Civil Service being the next best thing to the Church so far as his mother was concerned. None of the boys made the priesthood, though their sister Hannie became a nun and in the Listowel convent was known as Sister Gabriel.

At that time Mossie Walsh had never been out of Kerry and Listowel for him was a busy, interesting place, especially on market days and when the races were on. The boy loved it and the man never forgot it, returning again and again in later years to renew old acquaintances. He described it in many a story with great affection. Spillane's sweet shop, alas no more, was a favourite haunt of his youth, as was Broderick's bar round the corner from it when he was a bit older.

From the earliest dawn the fine old square – with its ivied Protestant Church in the middle – had been close-crowded with clumps of cattle, each guarded by two or three country lads – lean shrill-voiced fellows, armed with ash-plants that they used mercilessly on beasts that tried to break away or trespass – but now all the best cattle had been sold and railed: the polled-Angus crosses, the shorthorns, white-fronted Herefords, blue-and-white Fresians: and there were left only scattered remnants of throw outs, longhorns, frenchies. Here and there a felt-hatted dealer still moved from group to group, and high voices decried ridiculous offers or protestingly accepted equally ridiculous ones but for all practical purposes the sale was over.

The public-houses – and there are fourscore in that town – were reaping their brief harvest; for the breeders, having been paid for their cattle, were engaged in soothing long throats strained from hard bargaining, and no farmer would care to leave Listowel with, as they say, the curse of the town on him. Before each and every public-house was a row of red-painted, springless, country carts harnessed to donkeys, jennets, or short-coupled horses with remarkably clean legs; and the hum of the high-pitched Kerry voices came out from the bars like the song of the bees swarming.[9]

Listowel is still full of pubs, one kept by the inimitable John B. and Mary Keane among them, and of gay, warm, friendly people. Maurice Walsh is loved there still.

Life in Listowel and at Ballydonoghue around 1895 was not all shooting and fishing and tramping in and out to college. There was work on the farms at Ballydonoghue and Gunnsborough or wherever a neighbour needed a hand, as well as other pastimes. Mossie was

25

good with his hands, especially at carpentry, and made a fine bed of which his mother was very proud.

He had already a lively tongue and for all his short size (he was a bare five foot one at this time) had abundant vitality and dark good looks. He had no lack of girl friends, with the ready word and the quick smile for all of them, but in his late teens he fell in love hopelessly with his cousin Della O'Connell, a beautiful girl with soft, dark curly hair, the prototype for the darkhaired women who were to compete with the inevitable redheaded ones in his books. It was a hopeless love because they were first cousins and there could be no question of anything coming of the budding romance. That was the second touch of sadness in his life and it left him quieter and more withdrawn than he had been, for a time. Della's father, his uncle Tom O'Connell, gave him a lot of sympathetic understanding in those days and the kindly figure of bluff Tom Gayne in *Castle Gillians* is modelled in part on him.

Della eventually married the son of the Ballylongford baker O'Hanrahan. Mossie was not to marry an Irish girl at all, but the story of his great romance comes later.

Chapter 3. **The Burgeoning Writer.**

So far the picture emerging of the youthful Maurice Walsh is that of the lively son of a small farmer in the West of Ireland, clever but not quite clever or respectable enough for the Church; interested in outdoor activities, in boxing and swimming, in shooting and fishing; with a capacity for friendship, lasting and enduring friendship; and with the great benefit of devoted parents and a large and happy family. His was an uncomplicated life. His mother was pushing him towards the Civil Service but he was not particularly interested in that and if he did not make it there were plenty of other avenues and there was always the land.

Yet there was a lot more to the boy than that. He had always been an imaginative child, deeply impressed with the stories he had heard from his father and his father's friends since ever he could remember. From an early age he was a talented sketcher with pencil or crayon and excelled at horses and people's heads. He would sit quietly in the kitchen at Ballydonoghue for hours, with all the bustle of the family around him, sketching from pictures or from memory or even from life. On one memorable occasion a sergeant from the police cycled out from Listowel to see John Walsh about some question of straying beasts, a minor matter but one he saw fit to enquire into himself. He came into the kitchen and had a cup of tea and a scone or two but his business was soon concluded and the visit did not take long at all. As he got up to leave, young Mossie handed him a startlingly vivid likeness of himself, drawn while he had been sitting talking. It left him speechless, perhaps the only Irish policeman ever to have been so afflicted. Unfortunately, Maurice's drawings have not survived but the talent has and finds expression in the work of his grandson, the painter Manus Walsh whose craft shop at Ballyvaughan offers delicate work in enamel as well as paintings.

At an early age, too, it became clear that Mossie was particularly sensitive to atmosphere, to the aura of a place and to the sensitivities of people. That too was a facet of his character which stayed with him all through his long life, to the benefit of his books and the delight of his friends. He claimed to have seen ghosts on several occasions. It was not a matter to be made very much of, simply a fact of life in its many contours.

The first occasion was in the kitchen at Ballydonoghue while the family was saying the evening rosary. Mossie was about ten at the time and Elizabeth Walsh noticed his eyes shift suddenly to the stepladder going up into the loft where the hired man and the boys slept. He did not start or seem at all afraid, just intent. Elizabeth could see nothing there. John Walsh carried on saying the rosary and when it was finished, Elizabeth leaned over to her son.

"What were you looking at a while back, Mossie?" she asked.

"A grand old man coming down the ladder," he said, and went on to describe the man in great detail: face, hair, clothes and the way he hunched his shoulders. The description was that of an old herdsman, dead before Mossie was born, who had worked on the farm – and slept in the loft – when John Walsh was a lad. John Walsh, who remembered him with pleasure, was not in the least perturbed by the apparition and sought to attach no hidden meaning to it. It simply was.

On another occasion, a few years later, Mossie and his friend Jim Hennessy saw a woman kneeling in a ditch at the side of the road one evening but when they approached her she simply faded away. Jim was worried by it all and anxious to get away but Mossie was only interested and wanted to stay to see if she would reappear.

Later in life Maurice Walsh was never afraid of any intimation of the supernatural. Believing as he did that the aura of the place might well reach out to something aware in someone sib to it, he welcomed the contact. Once, when he was an exciseman, someone bet him that he would not have the nerve to stay overnight alone in a notoriously haunted house. He did stay and lay awake reading all night. No apparition appeared to haunt him but during the night his bedroom door opened briefly, as if in a draught, then closed again in the eddy. Long enough, he said, for something to take a look at him and go about its business.

There were two more personal incidents. The first occurred when his mother died in 1913. He was stationed in Scotland at the time and in the early hours of the night he felt a light touch on his forehead and distinctly heard his mother say, "I'm going, Mossie. Goodbye now."

He told his wife first thing in the morning that his mother had died and so it turned out. She died at 2 a.m. that same morning. When his father died in 1934, his wife heard the news first and went into his summerhouse-cum-study to tell him. He was looking out of the window and did not turn round or react when she told him. "I know it," he said quietly and would say no more.

With that sort of sensitivity, the background of stories and folklore and the influence of his father's books, it was not surprising that he began to write stories himself at a fairly early age. While he was still at school in the early 1890s, he had a story accepted by the old *Weekly Freeman* for publication in the Fireside Club section, run for children under the by-line of "Uncle Remus". Copies of the paper for this period are no longer available in the British or Irish National Libraries, but we know from Maurice Walsh himself that his successful story was a tale about bush ranging in Australia, heavily influenced by Rolf Bolderwood's *Robbery Under Arms*. It won him two guineas, the first of his literary earnings.

Apart from Bolderwood, Maurice Walsh as a boy used to read the works of Bulwer Lytton, the melodramas of "Monk" Lewis and the bold historical romances of G.P.R. James. That sort of fare, coupled with what he got from reading with his father, such as Robert Buchanan's colourful stories and rhymes, gave him an early taste and strong feeling for vigorous romantic fiction. Indeed George James's historical tales, and perhaps particularly *Richelieu: a Tale of France* and the linked French stories, were the main influences on the earliest of the stories he was to write as an adult, "Tearlath O'Daly of Dundareigh" which appeared in the *Irish Emerald* in 1908.

He was also reading Walter Pater when he himself was beginning to write poetry and at that time he had great enthusiasm for Pater's style, though in later years he was to think that Pater strove too hard for effect. "'Tis when we were young that his sound and fury – mostly stage thunder – astonished and delighted us."[10]

Maurice's early love of books came from his father but his respect for learning and the process of hard work needed to ensure that learning had depth and significance came from his mother Elizabeth, with the gentle help of Michael Dillon and the stern discipline of Morgan O'Flaherty. By the time he was seventeen and had begun to imbibe and construe these varied lessons, there were six younger brothers and sisters at home at Ballydonoghue, from the baby Julia (Jule) who was only four and could do what she liked with him, to Timothy (Tim) who was fifteen and whose head was full of the sound of fifes and drums and the sight of waving banners. Mossie decided that they were all too slack so he invaded the sanctuary of "the room", so long preserved for visitors and the priest in particular, and set up a blackboard there to ensure that the younger ones learned their lessons properly. He was very strict with them but his sister Bridget (Bridgie), who was two years older than he and their mother's mainstay in the house, used to step in when the little ones got tired or querulous. In later years, after Maurice's wife died, Bridgie kept house for him in Dublin. She had always been good at managing him and never lost the knack – or the authority.

Strict though Maurice was over lessons, he inspired great affection in his brothers and sisters and in his friends. They used to do little services for him without being asked for the pleasure of seeing him pleased. When eventually he had to leave home for the Excise Service, his departure caused enormous unhappiness. One of his friends, Tommy Costello, brought him a Happy St Patrick's Day handkerchief as a gesture and neither he nor Maurice was able to speak. Maurice always kept the handkerchief. It was out of that kind of simple but sincere and moving experience that Maurice Walsh drew the ideal of friendship and loyalty and affection that he was to write about so effectively thirty years later.

There he was then as the nineteenth century drew to a close, building around and in himself a store of impressions and memories, taking in the atmosphere and traditions of Kerry and its people that stretched back in storytelling through Murrough O'Connor and Hennessy's *Lays of Malharia* to the deeps of time. All that was fermenting inside him, waiting for the right moment to break out. Maurice himself always knew he would write but it was to be some years before the impulse bore true fruit. Which was just as well, since the experiences of those years were to contribute enormously to the range and depth of his books.

> I was always inclined towards writing, God help me, but I spent fifteen years in the Highlands – and the Lowlands where hae ye been – and did not write at all. Because I was living, see? Living. Neil Gunn and myself rambled the hollow lands and hilly lands and did a little work amongst the Highland stills, got to know a good whisky and fished and shot some in an honest and peaceful way – mostly.[11]

Mossie the Student, the farmer's son, was about to embark on the most decisive period of his life and become Mossie the Gauger.

Part 2.

Brewing

The Excise Service: British 1901 - 1922
Irish 1922 - 1934.

FORRES

Maurice Walsh in 1906.

Maurice Walsh at 39.

Chapter 4. **Entrance and First Postings.**

Elizabeth Walsh was determined that her clever eldest son should enter the Civil Service and that his brother Tim, two years his junior, should follow him. Paddy, who was six years younger again, would have the farm and the baby boy Mick would be provided for later. First, however, Mossie had to pass the examination.

He missed it at the first attempt through sheer lack of interest, but when he saw how much that upset his mother, he agreed to try again and to take it seriously. Even then he spent most of his time in Dublin reading Irish history rather than preparing for the examination. It was not an easy thing for him to buckle down to, as he had promised, for the twenty-one-year-old Kerryman already had strong views about the Irish heritage and, in particular, a growing antipathy to what he saw as the insensitive arrogance of the British Empire. The Boer War had started and Maurice Walsh was temperamentally much more inclined to join the Irish Brigade fighting for the Boers than to join the British Imperial Service. Nearly fifty years later and after two World Wars his views had not changed markedly and one of his great personal dislikes remained "the bloody British Empire, which you must not confound with the tight little island of England" and certainly must never equate with Scotland.

It was while he was in Dublin at this time that he began to think about an Irish historical novel set in the time of Hugh O'Neill's struggle against Queen Elizabeth. Nothing came of it at the time but the idea went on germinating in his head.

Whatever the distractions, he was successful in the examination, coming in the first fifty of two thousand candidates. He entered the government service on 2 July 1901 and was posted to Limerick as an Assistant Revenue Officer in the Customs and Excise Service.

His brother Tim, coming along after him, took the examination but failed in one question. While he was in Dublin for the occasion, Queen Victoria was over on her state visit and Tim was captivated by the sight of the Connaught Rangers on their big white horses providing the guard of honour. It raised all the old dreams of the bold soldier's life and he thought what grand times they must have. However, he went back to Kerry dutifully and like Mossie before him was sent back to St Michael's College in Listowel to prepare for another attempt at the entrance examination. One day soon after, however, a recruiting sergeant came to Listowel and the sound of fife and drum carried Tim away. He joined up there and then and was whisked off to Galway Barracks without being allowed home.

In the event Tim, who was usually known as Tadgh, did not like the army at all on his first acquaintance with it. He and a friend from Tralee who had joined with him found themselves increasingly lonely and one night simply decided to go home. They were soon missed and it was not long before they walked into one of the road blocks set up to stop them. It was a policeman from Ballybunion, practically a neighbour, who recognised Tadgh and had him sent back and Tadgh never forgave him. When the two boys were returned to barracks they were seen by the commanding officer himself and told him simply that they had been unbearably lonely. He turned out to be a very humane man who prescribed no punishment and wrote to their mothers to explain where they were and that, though naturally homesick, they were all right. Elizabeth Walsh began to mobilise her forces to get Tadgh out but the regiment was posted to South Africa before she could achieve anything.

Tadgh survived the Boer War unscathed though a comrade standing next to him had his head blown off. He got used to the army and quite liked it, even if at close quarters the fine white horses he had so admired in Dublin seemed both uncomfortable and awkward. He had never straddled a horse or donkey in his life until he joined the Connaught Rangers and after he left the regiment he never did again.

When the Rangers returned at last to Ireland, Tadgh had made a useful reputation for himself and there was the prospect of a commission in the offing if he stayed on. Elizabeth was having none of that. She wanted her son home and paid ten pounds to buy him out. As it happened, just at that time a new master was being sought for the Listowel workhouse and Tadgh's energetic uncle Paddy suggested he was the very man for the job. There was some diffidence at first because John Walsh was on the Board of Guardians and Tadgh's uncle Tom O'Connell was the chairman. Once that scruple was overcome, though, Tadgh clearly led the field of seven candidates and was duly selected. He made a great success of the job and was universally liked and respected. He was always known as "the Master", even after the workhouse itself was burned down in 1932 and never replaced.

His brother Mossie, established in the Civil Service, did not stay in Ireland very long. In that first year, 1901, he had been to Athenry for a spell (and thought a bit more about his historical novel, in the context of the sacking of that town) and a week before Christmas was down in Valentia Island when out of the blue came a short-term posting to the Ben Nevis distillery at Fort William in Scotland. It was a move of root-wrenching suddenness, for his family as well as for Mossie himself, to be shifted five hundred miles from Kerry in the depth of winter and "transplanted under Ben Nevis, that massive bulk shouldering above the mighty welter of mountains in Lochaber of Scotland".[12] According to Maurice himself the first man to meet him at the station there was from Clare – and he was drunk.

Thus began his introduction to the Scottish stills and to a land and people he was to come to love as his own. He was not left in Fort William very long on this occasion, however, and in 1902 found himself back in Ireland as an assistant in the Limerick area. The following year, 1903, saw him back in Scotland, in the Stirling Collection once more but this time for duty amongst the Lowland grain stills at Alloa, Carsebridge, Glenochil and Cambus. In 1904 he was attached to the Derby Collection for a two year stint with the English brewers but in 1906 he came to the Elgin Collection for work among the Highland stills once more. Speyside and Moray were to be his true home in the service. The Speyside Station

> ... included more than the basin of the Spey; it included the Deveron, the Fiddich, the Spey, the Lossie, the Findhorn and the Nairn, from Glenlivet – the real Glenlivet – to Inchgower, near Buckie, from Glendronach near Huntly, to Brackla at Cawdor. Into that soberly-rolling and chimney-stalked territory three dozen of us young fellows used gather for the distilling season from October to May, lads from all Scotland, England, Wales and Ireland, the four most quarrelsome nations in the world – but it was not blood that flowed.[13]

With those "young fellows" Maurice Walsh had found his own people. He had some postings outside Scotland after that but for the most part the remainder of his period in the British service was to be spent there.

What sort of man was Maurice Walsh by 1906? Physically he was five feet six inches tall, of medium build but deceptively slight looking with powerful shoulders and hands and lots of quick, explosive energy. His grey eyes were ever ready to sparkle and under a bushy moustache his pugnacious lower lip was more likely to twitch in a smile than a grimace. His dark, wavy hair was plastered down to look respectable but sprang up in a bush as soon as he forgot and ran his hands through it. He had drifted into the Excise Service to please his mother and found to his surprise that the life – and the company of his fellows – suited him down to the ground. His commitment to the service was total from the beginning. He admired its traditions and ideals and was to devote many hours of his own time to preserving them.

In nature he was easy going, generous to a fault with his friends and the friends of his friends, gay, restlessly energetic and insatiably curious about people and places, but even then showing the signs of resolution and determination and rigorous personal honesty that were the foundation stones of his character. He already had a developed code of personal integrity, of staunchness and friendship, which set very high standards for himself and for his friends and were to form the basis for the strong principles and ideals which would characterise his later life. He had from his father an innate sense of the fitness of people and of places and from his mother a strong moral sense of right and wrong. He was lucky, perhaps, that the colleagues he found in the Excise Service at that time matched up to his own standards and he never lost sight of the way they viewed life and work in those early years when later in his career he was trying to guide the officers' association of the young Irish service, Comhaltas Cana. He wanted its members to be what his friends and colleagues in the service at the turn of the century tried to be:

> . . . a loosely shackled friendship of men . . . who will do their day's work efficiently, because work should be done efficiently, and thereafter be brothers to a prince or fellows to a beggar, if found worthy; giving to Caesar the things that are Caesar's and to God the things that are God's – for, after all, there is but little due to Caesar.[14]

But of course everything was not couched in this high moral tone in the early days – or later. There was also devilment ready to brew up when the proper occasion allowed (and not infrequently when it did not) and always a developed sense of fun and of the exuberance of living. Maurice Walsh had shown the beginnings of these qualities in Kerry as a lad but it was in Scotland that they came to flower.

Chapter 5. **Scotland.**

From the very beginning Scotland touched Maurice Walsh where he lived, to use one of his own phrases. He found in the Scottish Highlands, in Speyside and the long, wide province of Moray, a country and a people with which he was wholly sib. A great aunt of John Walsh had married a man from Ballindalloch, Ivor Macpherson Grant, so there was some knowledge of the Scottish Highlands within the Walsh clan but nothing to prepare the young exciseman for the breadth and grandeur of the Highland scene. His first short posting introduced him to Long John.

> To put it as an understatement, there was nothing wrong with Long John's whisky. It stood up to age as well as Talisker itself. Maturing equably, say in a first-fill sherry cask, for twenty years in a cool, dark warehouse, yes, sir! there was nothing wrong with it.[15]

His first long stint in Scotland, however, began in 1906 with his transfer to the Elgin Collection. That introduced him to the great Highland malts and to Dufftown in Banffshire, a small Highland town whose principal occupation was the making of fine whisky and which was built not on seven hills like Rome but on seven stills. In the early part of the century, young, unattached excisemen working in the town's distilleries lived in a house near Glenfiddich Distillery called the Malt Kilns. It was run by an exciseman called Stewart in those days and later by his two daughters. Many the ceilidh was held there of an evening, with song and talk and whisky and more talk.

> We were really a friendly, easy-going, non-conforming community – distillers, brewers and revenue alike – and we were extra-ordinarily continent. Continence is the only way between a palate and malt whisky, and we were as continent as a connoisseur with a vintage claret. I knew one small town with seven distilleries and I knew an expert who could distinguish the seven by bouquet alone. These seven distilleries were in one mile of highland river; they used the same water, peat and malt, and the methods of brewing and distillation were identical, yet each spirit had its own individual bouquet. One, the best, mellowed perfectly in seven years; another, the least good, not a hundred yards away, was still liquid fire at the end of ten years.[16]

The expert with the marvellous nose was, of course, Maurice Walsh himself, though it took him several years to acquire the skill.

It was a lively time. The work was interesting and not confined to distilling supervision since there were pensioners to be interviewed too and dog and gun licences to be issued and renewed. In those days the Customs and Excise Service was responsible for those miscellaneous duties as well as the main excise work. In fact, the investigation of claims to the old age pension was a considerable task but one that Maurice Walsh and his colleagues enjoyed because it got them out and about and let them meet people, very often people with interesting, living memories of times and life styles long gone. For someone like Maurice Walsh, deeply interested in history and even more interested in people, that sort of thing was meat and drink.

Maurice ranged far and wide in Moray and left many traces. If you go today to the Glenburgie Distillery at Forres and ask to see the excisemen's room, you will find a large wooden cupboard full of forms and paper records. The insides of the big double doors are covered with the signatures of serving and visiting excisemen over many, many years. It is a significant historical document in itself and amongst the names it is easy to pick out the neatly written legend "M. Walsh, North Kerry".

For a time Maurice Walsh was gauger (excise officer) at the small Dallas Dhu Distillery at Dava on the edge of the great Dava moor. It was during this period that he met someone who was to become a great friend, Archie MacDonald of Tirriemore, Lochindorb, later to be immortalised as Archie MacGillivray of Loch Ruighi, in *The Key Above the Door*.

> Archie was a free man who acknowledged no ties, a fisher of note, a deadly shot, learned in all the lore of the hills and the clans, a man of strange culture and infinitely worth knowing. He had taught me all I know about rod fishing and the killing of fish. In all airts of the wind he knew where in the loch the best brown trout would rise to the fly, and even on days when no fish would rise, he had lures of his own that never failed us. . . . He was a long, lean man, with two or three bends in him like a gnarled birch tree, attired in the patched saffron-brown of the Gael, with deep-set blue eyes very much alive and a great mat of soft nut-brown beard hiding most of his face. One could learn nothing and everything from Archie's face.[17]

That was Archie in the book but as near as makes no difference Archie in real life too. He and his brother Jimmy stayed by Lochindorb, the Loch Ruighi of the story, with the same island holding the ruins of the Wolf of Badenoch's stronghold. The key of Archie's cottage was always on the ledge above the door if Maurice Walsh called and found the brothers out on the hill or on the loch and he would have the table laid and the kettle boiling by the time they got home. He might have called about the pension but no excuse was needed to stay the night, listening to some of the strange tales Archie had stored in his head or spending the night fishing the loch in Archie's boat the *Nancy*. After *The Key Above the Door* was published and became famous, Maurice Walsh visited Archie on one of his trips back to Scotland from the Irish Free State. Archie was delighted to see him but gave him a stern face at first.

"What for did ye pit me intil a book, Mr Walsh?" he asked. And as an aside to the others present, "The worst o't is, it's a' lees that's in it!"

One night Archie suggested a walk right up to the tops of the surrounding hills. It was a fine clear night with bright moonlight but the black moss at the heights looked as if it were studded with white bones and presented an eerie sight in the still evening. The "bones" were in fact the roots of trees of the old great Caledonian forest, thrown up to the surface and bleached white in the sun. Archie had many tales of the queer things that had been found in the hills and the queerer things that might still appear. It was the same with the loch. Most of the fish in Lochindorb were pretty small, though game, but Archie had found and preserved a backbone washed ashore at the southern end of the loch which was seven foot two inches long and a foot wide. No one knew what sort of fish it had been but there are strange things still in some of the Highland lochs, not just Loch Ness.

After Archie and Jimmy had died, their sister Jean went to stay at Tirriemore and Maurice Walsh had a great key made to hang over the door. He himself did not like to go back to the place after it had lost the spirit of Archie.

Many years later, in 1957, he wrote an account of a fishing expedition with the real Archie and paid moving tribute to this good friend and the long, easy days and nights spent with him among the hills and lochs.

The long oval of the loch was shining and wimpling under the evening sun and the evening breeze; the grey walls of the Wolf's castle stood out starkly against the shine; the bell heather was brilliant in the sunny hollows; and all the brown waves of the moors, one behind the other, seemed to be flowing down into the bosom of the loch. A wide and lonely land full of peace and aloofness.

For over all that far-flung expanse there was only one human habitation. On the north-western side of the loch a few scanty green fields had been won out of the leagues of heather, and above a clump of willows near the water, rose the white walls and blue slates of a farmhouse: the farm and homestead of Tirriemore, the domain of Archie MacDonald. Archibald MacDonald, Highland gentleman, brown-bearded like a doormat, blue-eyed like

Somerled, tall as a spear, massive handed, tough as steel, supple as a woodbine gad. Gaelic was his mother tongue. I have tried to keep him alive in that book I wrote, yet he is long dead and God rest him. And Tirriemore is empty, and Lochindorb lonely without him.[18]

Another good friend from this time was a colleague in the Excise, Percy Knight from Cornwall. Percy was a gay lad, enthusiastic, friendly and with a fine voice. Maurice Walsh could not sing a note but claimed always to have great tunes in his head. They used to fish and shoot some together and play golf with increasing skill. Maurice's handicap was nine. He played golf right handed, though he was in fact left handed and frequently used the word "kittog" or "kittoch", after the Irish "ciotóg", to sign articles in the association journal. Football and cricket were popular too and Maurice was a useful left handed bowler.

One year he and Percy went for a short climbing holiday in the Cairngorms, intending to spend the nights in a climber's cottage. On arrival there, however, they found it full of schoolboys to the point of bursting, so despite the fact that it was April and the nights were chill, they slept in the heather like many a hardy lad down the years before them. In the early morning when the sun was still weak they took the bold course to get the blood flowing and plunged into a loch near the cottage. Their yells woke the schoolboys but they were not too worried about that. For the next two days and nights they roamed the hills, living on a huge store of sandwiches and a liberal supply of malt. Maurice Walsh never liked sandwiches after that but there was no question of his going off whisky.

In this vigorous, lively but relaxed atmosphere it is not surprising that he began to think about writing again and mapped out some stories in the evenings when he was not at a ceilidh or engaged in fine disputation with his friends. It was something he always had in the back of his mind and if he could earn some extra money in the process it would be welcome. Maurice had never been poor but had never had any money to spare either. He started sending off stories and in 1908 had two published in the *Irish Emerald*, in the February and May issues. The first was a somewhat laboured melodrama, very old fashioned seeming to modern eyes, involving a mix up over jewels having to be sold to meet a business commitment and avoid ruin. It was called "Dick Clinton's Dilemma" and carried no hint of story-telling genius. The May story was very much better. "Tearlath O'Daly of Dundareigh" was a rousing tale of adventure in the time of Richelieu. It owed much of its subject matter and colour to the influence of the George James stories of the Richelieu period but nevertheless displayed a lively spirit and ingenuity of its own. Here was someone who could tell a tale.

Saulx-du-Sud, king of the road, grown weary of taking spiritless purses, offered his services to the Cardinal, king of men, against the Conde and the High Constable; and the Cardinal, in pressing need of despatch riders, wrote him a free pardon and gave him rank to lead a score of pikes.

The plot is slight but very well executed.

In July of 1908, however, the *Irish Emerald* printed the first instalment of a twenty part story entitled "Eudmon Blake, or The Sack of Athenree", which was an entirely different kettle of fish. The paper hailed it as

. . .one of the finest Irish historical stories ever written. Its time is that of Hugh O'Neill and Red Hugh Roe O'Donnell, when these two heroic chiefs were making so glorious a stand for Ireland against the forces of Elizabeth. It breaks new ground, however, not being concerned with the better known incidents in their careers but with the events leading up to that wonderful dash into Connaught of Red Hugh O'Donnell to punish the defection of certain chiefs, in the course of which he overran a large part of that province, burning the gates of Athenree, then in possession of the English, and pillaging the town, with that event as a climax.

The *Emerald* got over excited perhaps, but this is certainly a full blooded tale of wild and heroic deeds, with superb pace and vivid scenes. It had been taking shape in Maurice Walsh's mind ever since his days in Dublin reading the *Annals of the Four Masters* instead of studying for the Civil Service competition and now he was ready to set it down. It is a magnificent blood and thunder yarn which twenty years later was to be revised and recast by Maurice in the light of tried and tested experience in the storyteller's craft to become one of his best books and probably in truth what the *Emerald* called the first version, "one of the finest Irish historical stories ever written". That was *Blackcock's Feather*.

The year 1908 was an eventful one then for the budding writer. Maurice Walsh seemed set towards a literary career but the most significant event was a very different one. That year saw the publication of some of his stories but it also saw his wedding to Caroline Isobel Thomson Begg.

. . . . . .

Chapter 6. **A Red-Headed Woman and Her Twelve Sisters.**

Dufftown was and is a thriving little town built, as they say, on seven stills. The blue white smoke rises all around, drifting lazily into the air in the serene knowledge that all production there is legal and fully supervised and inspected by the officers of the Customs and Excise. It is a quiet town; traffic is not heavy apart from the big lorries that roll into and out of the distilleries. The main street is steep, climbing up steadily to the square and its cross roads, but it is spacious, wide by any standard and very broad indeed for a sleepy Highland village. But this is not just any village. It is Dufftown, where the very air and atmosphere spell whisky. The life of the town revolves round the whisky trade and it is no different in that respect today from what it was in 1906 or 1907. The people are courteous and friendly, used to the comings and goings of many strangers with business in the town and thousands more with only curiosity who flock through in the summer season to see where the "real" whisky is made. The major companies recognised this trend long ago and encourage visitors to tour the distilleries and to sample the "produce" before they leave. The best organised is undoubtedly Glenfiddich, where charming and knowledgeable lady guides shepherd their little flocks around the premises and answer their many questions. It seems particularly fitting that one of these, a delightful young lady called Helen Macleod, is the grandaughter of one of the sisters of the red-headed woman who married Maurice Walsh, the gauger.

The life and prosperity of Dufftown has long centred in the whisky trade and the people who come and go most, but nevertheless stay long enough in the town to get to know it (and let the town get to know them), are the excisemen. That was even more true in the early years of this century than it is today, and a mother with marriageable daughters in 1906 would look with interest on young, unattached excisemen as possible matches. Many such matches were made. Alexander Begg, a Dufftown auctioneer, had thirteen daughters (though not all of them survived childhood) and he and his wife thought that well behaved, respectable, batchelor excisemen were the salt of the earth.

The Begg household was a remarkable one. All the daughters, clever, vivacious girls, strong willed, proud, quick tongued and lively, were ruled very firmly by their remarkable mother "Grannie" Begg. Grannie was the prototype of them all and managed on little funds to send seven of them to college at a time when girls were destined for the kitchen rather than for an independent career. Caroline Isobel Thomson Begg was the eleventh of the thirteen daughters. Alexander Begg got a little desperate as the overwhelming tide of daughters continued to roll along and started giving them masculine sounding middle names as a sort of unconscious earth magic.

Caroline was always known as "Toshon" since that had been the nearest she could get to Thomson when she was a little girl and the mispronunciation stuck as a nickname. No doubt it suited Alexander Begg better, too. She was twenty in 1906, seven years younger than Maurice Walsh, and had just finished a course of training at the Church of Scotland Teacher Training College in Aberdeen. Her testimonial from the college covered drawing, singing, needlework and household management.

She was a beautiful, spirited girl, with delicate features, clear blooming skin, bright eyes and a great mass of magnificent red hair in whose meshes Maurice was soon entangled. The manuscript of *While Rivers Run*, Maurice Walsh's second book which was published in 1927, contains the dedication, "To Toshon, who has the loveliest curled red hair that ever was seen in day or dreams". Toshon herself was embarrassed by that, for all that they had been married nearly twenty years by then, and in the published version the dedication says simply, "To Tohson, who has red hair also". (The first edition misspelled Toshon's name, to her great annoyance. It was put right in the later editions.)

The Beggs lived in a big, three-storied house called Blinkbonny in Dufftown, on the corner of Stephen Avenue and Fife Street. Maurice Walsh later used the name for the central house in *Trouble in the Glen* and there, too, it was a happy house, ruled by a wise woman. Grannie Begg was a great organiser, a tall, commanding woman and the rock upon which the household rested. Her eyesight grew steadily worse as she got older and for the last twelve years of her long life she was virtually blind, but that did not stop her getting around Dufftown and certainly did not keep her in ignorance of anything of moment affecting her family. Her birthday was on 26 April, while Maurice's was on the 21st, so they soon began plotting to celebrate them together.

Musical evenings at Blinkbonny were one of the high spots of Dufftown social life in those early days and for years after. They were very popular with the excisemen and particularly with Maurice's friend Percy Knight whose rich baritone rose splendidly to the occasion. Percy married Caroline Begg's sister Bertha, who was always known as Bobbie — Alexander Begg's fixation again perhaps. Those musical evenings involved some pretty serious singing, by individuals and groups, with Schubert lieder and the like being the order of the day. Everyone had to do an individual turn which was listened to critically and applauded warmly – if applause was merited. Maurice Walsh, with a chronic inability to sing a note, should have been severely disadvantaged but was not. Grannie Begg liked him and came to his aid when it was his turn. He would dance an impromptu Irish jig to mouth music provided by Grannie herself, and at the last terrific kick, off would come one of his slippers to hit a picture on the wall and the whole room would collapse in laughter.

Caroline and Maurice were married on 8 August 1908 at the Roman Catholic chapel in Dufftown by Father George P. Shaw. Caroline had to be converted to Catholicism in order to marry Maurice. It was a big step for a twenty-two-year-old girl in those days in Protestant Dufftown. Grannie was clearly a bit suspicious but she liked Maurice and made no objection. Alexander Begg by now was looking for grandsons. Maurice's brother Tadgh came over from Kerry to be the best man. He had returned from his stint in the army and was settled in as master at the Listowel workhouse. He was the only other Walsh present but the excisemen were there in force.

It was a grand day for the wedding, one of those Highland summer days when the sky is an almost painful blue and the light is so clear that you can practically touch it. There was plenty to eat and drink, with whisky at the right price, as they say. (Even in the shops decent taxed malt was only three shillings a bottle.) Without much enthusiasm, Maurice carried a top hat two sizes too small and wore a frock coat, but of course the women carried the day.

The newly-weds were able to spend a few days in Dufftown after the wedding in a house called Netherwood near the Glenfiddich Distillery, but Maurice was under notice of transfer to Kirbymoorside in Yorkshire. In fact Maurice and some of the other excisemen were under a bit of a cloud at that time. A few weeks before, the level of discussion at the Malt Kilns one evening had gone beyond the white heat of reason into the red heat of anger and while the odd, relatively friendly boxing match in the house was not unknown, this time things went too far. A very angry Welshman took a swing at Maurice but missed and hit a fretwork on the wall, which broke. It took some time to untangle the ensuing melee, in which Percy Knight was one of those involved, and in the investigation they all got a strong dressing down and the surveyor had them dispersed. Maurice was transferred to Kirbymoorside.

In the event, though, he and Caroline were happy there in a very pretty cottage with roses all round the door, but after a year Maurice was moved again back to Ireland, to Ballaghadereen in County Roscommon. By that time Caroline was expecting their first child so she went back to her mother in Dufftown where a son Maurice was born in June 1909. Maurice had left strict instructions that if the

Caroline

The Wedding

child were a boy, he was to be called John after his own father. Toshon, on her own and lonely and in love, took the strong course and disobeyed him. Grannie Begg was in on it too. The same Father Shaw who conducted the wedding ceremony baptised the child. It was customary at Catholic christenings in the Highlands at that time to put a pinch of salt in the baby's mouth representing the "salt of knowledge". They reckoned without Grannie Begg, however, who was there to hold the baby and see that no papist tricks were pulled. She was horrified when salt was put in the child's mouth and indignantly sucked it out again. Ever since then the family have been trying (without the slightest success) to prove that Maurice is not as bright as the rest of the family because of that incident.

Caroline and the baby soon joined Maurice in Ireland and in 1911 they were transferred once more, to Templemore in County Tipperary where a second son, Ian Alistair, was born. Much of the work at Templemore was concerned with the investigation of claims to the old age pension and Maurice used to hire a jaunting car to take him into the hills to interview claimants. He described such a trip in one of his stories, and the investigation itself.

We hard bitten Irish Pension Officers had developed a technique of our own in dealing with our aged but not simple countrymen. Certain answers to innocuous seeming questions, a tone of voice, a lift of eye, a shift of shoulder, and we knew Satan was at work. [19]

One day when Maurice was out delivering pensions Toshon bought and cooked her first steak for his meal. She was quite excited about it and prepared it very carefully, timing the operation so that it should be ready virtually when he walked in the door. Unfortunately he was two hours late. An increasingly anxious Toshon kept adding a little Worcester sauce to keep the steak moist. When Maurice did arrive at last he was a bit abstracted and said nothing when the plate was put in front of him.

"How do you like the steak, Mossie?" asked Toshon at last.

"It's tough," he said.

Toshon burst into tears and Maurice could not understand why.

They left Templemore when Ian was only a few months old and moved back to Scotland, where from 1913 to 1922 Maurice was the Attached Officer at Forres 2 General Station in Nairn District, Inverness Collection. His duties covered distillery work, dog and gun licences and some four hundred old age pensioners. Those years were very happy ones, with one exception. They had a daughter, Mary (Molly) Myron Walsh, on 20 January 1915 and were delighted with her. She was a beautiful child but she died of meningitis in 1918.

Caroline was heartbroken. A third son, Neil, was born on 9 January 1919 and Maurice was pleased that Caroline had him and relieved that it was not another girl, since it was too soon after the loss of Molly to be borne. According to one close relative, Caroline's niece Dorothy, Maurice himself showed little emotion but his dark hair began to turn grey within a week of the child's death.

Those years at Forres provided Maurice Walsh with a store of impressions and memories of Scotland that he never lost and on which he was able to draw vividly all his life. The family stayed first at Pilmuir Villas, which they rented from John Forsyth, the butcher, and where Maurice had a room as his office, and later moved to a house called Montana. They were living in Forres House by the time Maurice left Scotland.

He soon began to make his mark and it was said that people took out gun licences in his area just because he was such a gentleman. The Walshes soon had a wide circle of friends, both in the Excise Service and outside it. Percy and Bobbie Knight were at Elgin, virtually on their doorstep, and Dufftown itself was only thirty miles away (though in those days that meant a fair journey). Maurice and Toshon had lots of visitors, both casual and by invitation, though their evenings tended towards lively discussion rather than the musical extravaganzas which Grannie Begg was still organising at Blinkbonny.

At Forres House, Maurice would cough and get up after a bit. That was the signal for all the men to rise and go out to the kitchen for a dram. That was the invariable custom, a mixture of gentility in not taking a drink in front of the ladies and possibly also a little concern over the illegality of some of the supplies. Toshon herself would take a little whisky with plenty of soda when she and Maurice were alone of an evening. Since the whisky was free and she had to buy the soda she felt a bit guilty about using so much of it and used to water the soda down when Maurice was not looking!

It was a very healthy environment for the children to grow up in, with wide spaces and clean air. Maurice, the oldest son, was soon fishing and shooting with his father and an apt pupil he turned out to be. As a parent Caroline was probably stricter than Maurice, although Maurice set the tone and the standards for the family. On one occasion young Maurice had been given half-a-crown, a very large sum for a boy at the time, and in a wave of enthusiasm and excitement had spent the lot. The Presbyterian in Caroline was shocked at this irresponsible splurge and she brought the boy to tell his father what he had done. Mossie was in the garden digging when the irate Caroline and her crestfallen son arrived. Young Maurice explained to his father what he had done with the money and waited with some trepidation for the verdict and the punishment. His father was quiet for a few moments, then said, "God, boy, that was damn fine spending!" Young Maurice stole away very quietly from the ensuing row.

Mossie was still playing golf, at the Muiryshade course near the Forres Hydro and was honorary secretary of the Forres Golf Club. He won the Captain's Prize (a silver rose bowl) with a round which contained some unbelievably lucky shots. During the 1914-1918 War he saw war service along the coast — and poached the teeming Sanquhar Estate without a qualm to keep his family well supplied when food got short.

All these factors mashed and jelled and were stored away to be transmuted into sparkling prose years later. However, if there were one event at this time which could be regarded as having the greatest significance it was Maurice's meeting with Neil Gunn, who was sent to him at Forres as an unattached officer. There began then a friendship which was to last their lifetime. In the early days Neil Gunn used to join Maurice and Percy Knight on their shooting and fishing forays, especially those to the Lochindorb country.

There were three of us, one from Caithness, one from Cornwall, one from Kerry, Celts everyone – and, two or three times a month, from May to October, we fished a moorland loch on the first swell of the Highlands at the top-end of the county of Moray. We used take the evening train from Forres to Dava, a slow collar-straining, up-hill pull amongst pine woods and thin-skinned farms into the heart of the austere moors, a thousand feet above sea level. At Dava we took to the heather for a five mile tramp amongst the brown slopes.

That particular evening in July we set out for our moorland loch. Two went up by train as usual, but at that time I had acquired at second-hand (or it might be fourth) a unique motor-cycle, an F-N – Fabrique Nationalle des Armes de Guerre – that was shaft driven and sometimes achieved a speed of thirty knots under favourable conditions downhill. I told my friends that I would wait for them at Dava while I smoked two pipes, but not a moment longer. At Dava they waited ten minutes for me. On a sandy-brown track, in single file, we twisted hither-and-yon amongst the brown slopes. A cock grouse exploded from a heather clump, told us violently to "go-back, go-back", and floated on stiff pinions over a round summit. We ignored that command, climbed a final slope between quaking peat hags, and there was our loch, shining below us.[20]

In no time at all they would have rooted out the inimitable Archie and soon Percy's easy baritone would be regaling them with a ditty as they set up their rods and prepared to enjoy themselves.

These three and the F-N motorbike went straight into *The Key Above the Door* and Neil Quinn in the story, though described as an Irishman, was soon recognised as Neil Gunn. Neil and Maurice grew very close. They were both intelligent, articulate, natural mystics and keen sportsmen. Both wanted to write. The contours of their minds (and perhaps the configuration of their souls) fitted in an exceptional way. They used to discuss their ideas for stories and frequently exchanged plots. Neil Gunn suggested much of the form of Maurice's second book *While Rivers Run* and was his severest and best critic. The book *The Road to Nowhere* (1934) is dedicated to Neil and *The Hill Is Mine* (1940) to Neil's wife Daisy. Neil Gunn wrote about Maurice and Toshon specifically in *Off in a Boat* and obliquely in Chapter 37 of his autobiography *Atom of Delight*: "The man and his wife were my closest friends."

Up to 1922 they were very close and often in each other's company. After 1922 they continued to correspond frequently and met when they could, but that had to be less often since Maurice had volunteered to return to Ireland for service in the administration of the Irish Free State.

. . . . .

Chapter 7. **The Irish Free State.**

Maurice Walsh's father John had been a pro-Britisher but Maurice's own sympathies were never in doubt. He believed very strongly in Ireland as a nation and in Irishmen as distinct from Englishmen or Scotsmen or any other inhabitants of the Empire or the world – and woe betide anyone who forgot that. His own joking reference about wanting to go off and fight for the Boers instead of joining the Civil Service was only half a joke, although Maurice was always careful to distingush between the British themselves and their Empire. Or their "bloody Empire" as he was more likely to say.

There was one revealing incident in Forres in 1916, soon after Easter and the Rising in Dublin. A tight-lipped, white-faced Maurice Walsh peremptorily ordered a senior colleague out of his office, which happened to be in his own home. The surveyor who was, alas, an Irishman had made some belittling and hostile remarks about the 1916 men. He thought Maurice was far overstepping the mark and had no right to order him out of the office – probably he was right – but ejected he was anyway, forcibly. There was a great row and furious complaints and threats of disciplinary action from the surveyor but he got no joy at all because the collector at Inverness, to whom the complaints were addressed, very sensibly sat on the whole thing until it died down.

At the Armistice in 1918 Maurice caused a sensation in Forres by flying a special flag from his house. The effect was the more pronounced as that house sits in an imposing position upon a little hill. Maurice would have been delighted to fly a Scottish flag, the lion on a gold background, but the shops in Forres were all sold out of flags and materials. There was no way he was going to fly the Union Jack so Toshon and one of her nieces made an Irish flag, a harp on a blue background (the green background to the Irish flag was to be introduced later).

Maurice's own position in the politics of Ireland was not at all clear. On the one hand, he worked for the British Customs and Excise Service and was bound by his oath in that respect. He stood aloof from active involvement in the activities of, for example, the Irish republican movement of the early years of the century. Being stationed in Scotland perhaps made that easier for him than it might otherwise have been, for his sympathies lay very much with the republicans. His cousin Paddy Pat Walsh of Gunnsborough was one of the organisers of the Ballydonoghue Sinn Féin Club and the Fianna Éireann squad. Tom Dillon, his old teacher's son and his friend, was busy teaching Irish and lecturing on the 1916 Rising. Maurice's cousin Paddy organised the Ballydonoghue Company of the Irish Volunteers in 1918 and was killed by the Black and Tans at Gortaglanna, near Cnucanor, on 12 May 1921. He and three others were coming home from a mission one night, unarmed, when they were arrested by the Tans, lined up in a field and gunned down. Paddy Walsh, Patrick Dalton and Jerry Lyons were killed but a fourth man, Con Dee, made a run for it and escaped, although seriously wounded. It was Con who was able to tell the story. Maurice's youngest sister Julia, who was a nurse at that time and who married a well known republican Maurice Harnett, used to go with Doctor Enright from Listowel to where Con Dee was in hiding to tend his wounds. Norah Walsh of Tullamore who was captain of the Cumann na mBan went with some of the other girls to Listowel Barracks to claim the bodies. The funeral was a massive affair broken up by the Tans. At Gunnsborough they had in a frame behind glass a tuft of grass with Paddy's blood on it, a macabre touch but they were macabre times. Bryan MacMahon, the Listowel writer, wrote a long poem about the massacre called "The Valley of Knockanure" which has been set to music and is widely sung in Ireland still.

When the Free State was formed in 1922 Irishmen were asked to return to help and Maurice Walsh had no hesitation about volunteering, although Toshon was very much against it. She wished to stay in Forres where they were happy, with Blinkbonny and her family not far away. Maurice promised to bring her back on holiday, every year if she wished, and he would start writing again to pay for that. In any event off he went to Dublin on his own since fighting was still going on at that time. Caroline and the boys were to follow later. His colleagues in the Excise gave him a piano on his departure from the British service and that followed on with his family. Dublin was a wreck at the time from Nelson's Pillar up O'Connell Street with several areas of destruction down the quays.

Maurice was living at first at 6, Leinster Square, Rathmines, near the Portobello Barracks, at a house belonging to a music teacher at one of the Rathmines schools. Herr Scherrer became a good friend though the Walsh family soon had a little rhyme about his bald head: "Herr Scherrer has a fair share of hair."

Maurice was convinced he was doing the right thing but he missed his family a lot. He wrote a revealing letter to his sons at this time. It is dated Wednesday, 20 December 1922, just before Christmas, and is unmistakably Maurice Walsh speaking.

To Maurice, Ian and Neil Forbes Walsh,
  who are three Turks and Playboys.
    Your dad was very glad to get your letters and would have liked

them twice as long and three times as full of news. I am sure that you are very good boys to mother. Mother tells me that you are good boys but then if you were bad boys she would not like to tell me so because I would be so very sorry to hear that you were bad, and also because I would skin you alive, scalp you, and feed you to the Lion, the Tiger and the Dangeroos as soon as ever you set foot in Dublin. We stand no nonsense in Dublin. Even the small boys in the street shoot each other here, or at least they hold mock court martials and carry out the sentences in full detail – same as your mock elections. I heard as I passed, the claims of one urchin to be the rebel who was to be tried. But he was rejected because he did not know how to die. All the wee boys have little pistols that crack a cap quite loudly and they are always trying to frighten their elders by cracking a cap close behind. Only the Dublin people are not easily frightened. That's the kind of place Dublin is. It is more than twice as big as Forres and the bit that would be left over would be more than twice as big as Aberdeen. The station I am trying to get is called Chapelizod. It is just outside the town, or city and near the River Liffey – a river about the size of Findhorn. There are trout in that river, too, and dead cats and old tin-cans, so that when you'd be fishing you would always be catching something, and sometimes you would not be thanking God for what you would be catching. One man told me that in a spate he caught 30 trout all over a pound in weight. Being a fisherman myself, I believed that man. So gather up all the rods and tackle carefully and see that they are packed. Near Chapelizod too is one of the gates of Phoenix Park and the size of that park is 1800 acres. All of Forres House parks are only 24 acres, so you can understand how big it is. There are great flocks of beautiful deer grazing on it and on Sundays there are crowds of boys and men who play football and hurley (that is called shinty in Scotland and is the rough parent of hockey.) At one corner of the park is the Zoo, full of wild animals and small boys who are as wild as the animals. For when you'd be seeing a small boy like Ian or Neil staring at a monkey and both of them with their mouths open with surprise you could not tell which was the boy and which the monkey.

There are no boy scouts, as far as I know, but there are big hills near by which we will climb, and at every street corner there is an old woman selling apples – lovely red apples which the old lady polishes by spitting on them and rubbing with an intimate portion of her garments. The apples have a good taste however.

And that is all I will tell you about Dublin now. If you want more then write to me again and I will find out more things about this place. Tell mother that I do be thinking about her once or twice a day anyway, and that I have no news today, only that I am thinking of running down to Kerry on Friday evening to see my father who owns a farm and 17 cows, 3 horses, 2 goats and 11 donkeys besides pigs without number and the grace of God as well.

Maurice did in fact get the station he sought, the Phoenix Park Distillery at Chapelizod. It had been silent (i.e., it had ceased production) since 1921 but the bonded warehouses were full and methylation (to provide duty free spirit for industry) took place once a month. He was to be in charge there until his early retirement from the service in 1933. The first few years of organising the Irish Excise Service were pretty hectic and Maurice himself was very soon involved in the budding officers' association, Comhaltas Cana, as will be described in the next chapter. In 1922 and 1923, however, it was not at all clear how the new organisation was to develop and an air of complete unreality hovered over all because of the curfew. Moving about the streets of Dublin after dark in those days was a chancey affair but Maurice was fortunate in his digs. Herr Scherrer and his two sisters were very pleasant people who tried hard to make him feel at home. It was inevitable, however, that time in the evenings would hang heavy and it was that, coupled with an understandable nostalgia, that led Maurice Walsh back into writing.

In 1922, for my sins, I transferred to the service of the Irish Free State, left my family in Scotland and came to Dublin in the middle of a pleasant little civil war we were running at the time. I knew no-one in Dublin after an exile of so many years. There was a good deal of sniping after nightfall and being a cowardly man, I stayed indoors after closing time and read and read and read. That was the time that a sniper used an elm tree at the back of the digs for a nightly perch and we put on it a notice "Snipers will be prosecuted" and the sniper, with a sense of humour, moved to a tree in the next block.

I got tired of reading and I thought I might pass the time by trying to recall the glamour of Scotland, so I wrote *The Key Above the Door,* all about the province of Moray and the Isle of Skye. Who the characters are I'm not saying. Some say Neil Gunn and myself and Percy Knight and Jack Brereton, who is now in heaven, or there ain't one. I wrote it in three months and when we had settled down my wife and I typed it with two fingers – one each. And it lay about. Then a big British publisher offered a prize of £500 for a first novel and my wife, bold as brass, sent in our ewe lamb – for sacrifice. Yes, sir. The typescript was returned in three weeks without a single remark, not a single word of thanks or regret or abuse. Gorhhh! What a helluva yarn it must be, says I. And it lay about. Then one day a friend, Peter O'Donovan, was talking about writing a novel – he still is – and I said in a casual way "Dammit, anybody can write a novel, I wrote one myself" and he laughed at me and like another Thomas had to see [the] dog-eared manuscript and he read it in one sitting and liked it and said "The firm for you is Chambers of Edinburgh. This is their country and they give the new writer a show." So we sent it to Chambers and the great George Morris gave it a show and a chance. And you know how the chance came off. And J. M. Barrie wrote me a fine letter and I don't know how many tens of thousands the book has sold. After that, Chambers and I teamed up. Between us we have produced fifteen books and the wolf is kept well over the horizon, mostly.[21]

The competition referred to was one run by John Lane. *The Key Above the Door* appeared first in *Chambers Journal* as a serial between December 1925 and May 1926 and was published as a book in July 1926. It is interesting to record that Neil Gunn made it first into *Chambers Journal* with an article entitled "John o' Groats" in the issue of January 1925.

In this early period, though, Maurice Walsh also had three stories published in *The Dublin Magazine*. The first of these was "A Woman Without Mercy" which came out in the issue of December 1923 (Vol. 1 No 5). Essentially the same story was printed as "Face of Stone" in 1936 in the *Elk Magazine* in America with rather good illustrations by Harvey Dunn and in *Chambers Journal* in 1937. It was an early version of the first part of the book which was to appear in 1938 as *Sons of the Swordmaker*. It had become a much better story by that time.

The second story in *The Dublin Magazine* appeared in August 1924 (Vol. 2 No 1) and was called "The Mission Sermon", an interesting period piece which introduced Christopher Columbus in a minor role and was notable for the invention of a new coin, the "tassie par". The manuscript title of the story was "Pay Heed You Sinners" but that was dropped as potentially misleading. Liam O'Flaherty's "The Flood" appeared in the same issue. The year 1924 was an interesting one in the literary world. George Fitzmaurice had published his one act comedy *The Linnaun Shee* and Lord Dunsany produced *The King of Elfland's Daughter*. Neil Gunn made his first appearance in *The Dublin Magazine* that year with "The White Hour" (Vol. 1 No 8).

In January 1925 (Vol. 2 No 4) there was an interestingly constructed if macabre monologue entitled "A Dialogue". Mossie the Gauger was making his mark as Mossie the Author even before his first novel was accepted. The editor of *The Dublin Magazine*, Seamus O'Sullivan, was much impressed with this new writer and the wide range of subjects covered by him. He met Peter O'Donovan one day and said to him, "That friend of yours must be a marvellously travelled man."

Peter laughed. "Maurice?" he said. "He's never been out of Dublin in his life." That was a bit of an exaggeration, though not much, but it ruined Maurice with *The Dublin Magazine* and he had no more pieces published there.

Maurice was always very good at convincing evocations of place, even places he himself had never seen. In *The Key Above the Door*, for example, he has some striking passing references to Spain – "the long valley of the Madura where the white houses are strung along the river" and again, "the grey windy towers of El Greco and the thin waters of the Manzanares" – which say very little but give a strong impression of familiarity with the country referred to. Bryan MacMahon, the Listowel writer, told me that he thought that one of Maurice Walsh's great strengths as a storyteller was the ability to pick the bones out of a situation, particularly a historical situation, without the need for extensive research and yet make the resultant description indubitably authentic and convincing.

In February 1923, when Dublin was much quieter, Maurice went back to Scotland for his family. There was still some trouble in the south at that time and peace did not come finally until the August of that year, but it seemed safe to bring Toshon and the boys over to Dublin. The family stayed at first at Webb's Hotel at the back of the Four Courts, but before long they secured a house near Chapelizod, Number 4, St Michael's, Sarsfield Road, Inchicore. It was one of a terrace of four tall three-storied houses. There were long stairs up to a big attic with a billiard table, which was fine for the boys (and Maurice), but although the family lived there for nine or ten years, Toshon never liked it. Maurice made a summerhouse there of rough, unplaned wood but it was very snug and he used it to write in when he could. He used to write for a bit in the evenings and then put a white card in the window. That was the signal to his neighbours, all working in their gardens but keeping an eye on the Walsh summerhouse, to come and have a dram.

Another exciseman, Jack Spears, lived at Number 1, St Michael's. Peter O'Donovan, whom Maurice first met at Chapelizod, thought at the time that he might be in love with Jack's pretty daughter Norah. He was very bashful about it though and Norah herself simply ignored him. Maurice made up a little poem about the situation and gave it to Peter.

My love she lives at Number one,
My heart is at her door.

But when I call to see my love,
I call at Number four.

Peter was then and remained a very good friend, devoted to Maurice. He himself started to write a novel and the opening sentence was, "It was a very wet morning and there was only a handful at my funeral." He never got any further, although he did get into print later in the *Saturday Evening Post* with a piece about his friend Maurice Walsh.

St Michael's was always full of visitors, local or over from Scotland. Herr Scherrer and his two sisters would come to tea all the way across Dublin from Rathmines and he invariably was asked, and agreed, to play Weber's "Invitation to the Dance". Once they called when only young Ian was at home and though he never thought to offer them tea he did remember to ask Herr Scherrer if he wanted to play "Invitation to the Dance" before he went away.

Another regular visitor was a exciseman named Hugh Forbes whose name and physical characteristics Maurice used in *The Small Dark Man*. The Walshes had known him in Scotland where he had lodged with them for a time, and their third son was called Neil Forbes Walsh. He came back to Ireland at the same time Maurice did. He was small and dark, with immensely broad shoulders, a delightful man who sang Irish songs in a great deep voice. He too married a red-headed woman but he died within a few years of a disease of the middle ear.

Maurice Walsh was forty-three years old when he returned to serve the Irish Free State, a bit quieter than he had been when he went off to Scotland twenty years before, a settled man with family responsibilities, a wife and three sons to provide for.

> Ay, he was beginning to feel old, for he was at the far side of thirty, and at that age and for the next ten years, a man is at his oldest, his youth and agility behind, and the weight of years facing down on him. A man begins to assort himself to circumstances at forty-five or so and he is not old again until he cannot lift a sheaf o' corn, as the saying goes.[21]

Mind you, Maurice was seventy when he wrote that. At forty-three he was in fact just entering on his most prolific period of writing, coupled with a very deep involvement with the excisemen's association and a busy social life. He had always an aura of kindliness and friendliness and had the ability to put people at ease and make them smile in the most difficult situations, even lying on the floor at Rathmines with Herr Scherrer and his sisters while the bullets were flying outside. That was a very important part of his personality and one that became more strongly defined the older he got.

He was still very much an outdoor man, roaming the Wicklow Hills with his sons whenever he could get away. He had always been a great sporting man but after his return to Ireland he gave up shooting completely and would not kill anything. Fish were different.

Maurice remained at Chapelizod until his resignation from the service on 21 November 1933. The volunteer agreement under which he had, with others, returned to Ireland involved parity of pay and conditions with the United Kingdom service and a guarantee of the option of retirement on full pension if conditions were changed. In the very difficult economic conditions obtaining after de Valera came to power in the elections of 1932, a salary cut was introduced for the government service which clearly did alter the conditions for those Irishmen who had come back under the volunteer terms. The government resisted retirement on full pension by those who claimed entitlement to it but that decision was fought in the courts and the government lost. After the decision Maurice Walsh and others opted to go out on pension.

Maurice was in a curious position over that. He had always been pro-de Valera and very friendly with a number of people prominent in Fianna Fáil, especially Frank Aiken and Paddy Little. He had no contacts with Cumann na nGaedheal which was to become Fine Gael. His son Ian drove a car for Fianna Fáil in the 1932 election to take people to the polling station. Maurice certainly knew the circumstances leading to the salary cut and understood fully why such a drastic measure was thought to be necessary. On the other hand, he was a senior member of the officers' association, Comhaltas Cana, an immediate past president no less, and had a particular duty to do what was right for his colleagues, to give a lead and to be seen to stand up for his convictions. His well developed moral sense of what was right and fitting and what was wrong left him with little option and out on pension he had to go. The pension then was £376 per annum, though he knew he could supplement that amount by his earnings from writing. His fifth book was about to be published and his first story in the lucrative *Saturday Evening Post* appeared that same year, 1933. It was a considerable step, however, and Toshon was very worried about it even if Maurice showed no sign of anxiety.

Chapter 8. **Comhaltas Cana.**

When Maurice Walsh returned to Dublin, the Irish Customs and Excise Service was beginning to reorganise itself. J. J. Waldron was president of the excise officers' association, Comhaltas Cana. He wrote to Maurice early in 1923 asking him to help and help was immediately and unstintingly given. At any time Maurice Walsh was willing to sit down to prepare a letter or build up a case for the association and he very soon found himself holding office, as editor of he association yearbook, *Cainiris*, and successively as assistant general secretary, general secretary and president. While he was secretary in 1924-1926, J. J. Waldron was president and Eugene O'Connor was treasurer.

Maurice Walsh had a particular quality, recognised widely among his colleagues as well as by his family and friends, and that was the indefinable element in a human being that draws other people to him. It was partly his natural friendliness that made initial and continuing contact an easy and pleasant experience, but even more it was his personal warmth and evident integrity. He believed in the service and in its association and everyone could see that he did. People trusted him and that was immensely important. The early years of the Comhaltas were not easy ones as different ideas, often very strongly held, fought for mastery. Maurice was a natural healer of rifts, the constant standard to whom all could and did turn in crisis. More than one Comhaltas member has recorded incidents where it was through Maurice Walsh's mediation that critical periods were weathered. On one occasion, graphically described in the association journal *Irisleabhair*, there was a particularly serious dispute in the executive that could not be resolved. The whole committee adjourned to Maurice's house where he fed them and gave them a drink and made them discuss everything but the main issue, insisting that they keep right off it. "Before that night was out – it was morning – we all agreed that everyone else was right and that we were alright . . . ."[22]

The first and second issues of *Cainiris*, the Irish Customs and Excise yearbook, were produced by Maurice Walsh who used to say that *Cainiris* was in fact his first published book. It played a significant part in pulling the new service together.

The work certainly kept him very busy, as he told his publishers after *The Key Above the Door* had appeared as a serial in *Chambers Journal* and was about to come out in book form.

You are certainly treating *The Key Above the Door* with every consideration and I can only hope the result will not prove a loss to you. I very readily agree to give you the first offer of the next three novels that I write. . . . Unfortunately, I have not had much time for literary work. Serving the Irish Free State and my own Civil Service Association has kept me busy for a year but I hope to have an easier official time from now onwards. [23]

He was at that time working on *While Rivers Run* but in fact he continued to be kept very much involved in Comhaltas work on reorganisation proposals, trying to secure the best interests of the officer grade and preparing the association case for a special service commission (the Brennan Commission). His attitude to Comhaltas work was serious and concerned but never in an arid or humourless way. It is well illustrated by a letter he wrote to the membership in *Irisleabhair* at a time when there was much argument about membership drives and insistence on prompt payment of subscriptions. Both were important issues for the association but the way Maurice Walsh intervened was illuminating. The open letter is worth reproducing in full.

Too much preaching causes heedlessness, too much persuasion instils doubt, too much propaganda is met with indifference, too much reiteration of the truth makes lying pleasant. Our bleak coldness towards heaven and cheerful indifference towards hell are due to the unnecessary emphasis laid on the joys of the one and the warmth of the other.

Take our Comhaltas. Fundamentally, it is a voluntary Association. We are making it a conscript one. That latter is an undoubted fact, as the Executive knows. How many of our members have that thirty shillings extracted from them while they are backed into a corner?

If a man, who is a mite careless, knows that he will have any number of reminders, he will frequently fail to act on even the final one. There is really no need for strong-arm work. The Comhaltas officials need not and should not resort to frenzied and unheeded appeals. Most of us Officers know the absolute necessity for association. Why curse it! We must know. The few that do not must be fools. Let us run the Comhaltas on lines of austere voluntariness, with an invincible confidence that the man who believes will pay what is needed — today or tomorrow or next year, according to the nature of him. Let us say to everyman once:- "Here is your Association. It is needed. Join it when you are ready. Meantime we will carry on and get you as many benefits as we can, maintain our rights if we are able, and save you from degradation if possible. We will entertain you with a Journal and direct you with a Year Book. We know you will pay your subscription now or later on because – well, because you are a decent fellow, and sometimes a decent fellow is careless and a little improvident, but never a mean hound."

I do believe we would thus achieve a ninety percent membership. The other ten should not be accepted, even in a political party. A hundred percent membership can be achieved only through despicable fear and degrading greed, and we are now in danger of holding up these false gods and using the violent gestures of old Jonah, threatening the Babylonians.[24]

"Invincible confidence" in the decency of his colleagues was one of Maurice Walsh's great strengths as an officer of the association and a similar confidence in the decency of his fellow men made him an exceptionally tolerant man. He was a very successful general secretary and president because he cared deeply about the preservation of the ideals of the service and of the association, the ideals recognised and admired and resolutely supported from his earliest days in the Excise, among "the loosely shackled fellowship" he loved so much, men "cultured, philosophical, unprejudiced, unbribable, uncowable, a little irascible at times, a little cynical in spite of themselves, sardonic on occasion and not blinded by too much hope or any fear . . ."[25]

He took many opportunities to put that message over, whether it was in general council reports, personal conversations, letters to the journal or even reviews of works published by colleagues, such as the very encouraging and supportive review he wrote of Padraic Trimble's book of verse, *Irish April*.

This Service of ours, though it may be obsessed with the possibly sordid duty of assessing and collecting revenue, has never been wholly possessed by that duty. Which is a good thing. One might think that our every-day work would induce in us materialism, cynicism, and a general hopelessness in the spirituality that this Christian nation is supposed to be dowered with; yet the Customs and Excise has always been noted for its poets, visionaries, romanticists, and epicurean philosophers, and has gained in stature therefrom – and in actual material worth. And it is good to note that our young generation, Irish to the core, promises to better the old one in vision and culture.[26]

The association lost a very good member when Maurice Walsh went out on pension and the association knew it. His old friend Humphrey Kerins, the Comhaltas president at that time, launched a service wide appeal on behalf of the Executive Committee to mark the retirement with a special presentation. "The number of subscribers," he said, "will be considered more important than the amount of the funds, and subscriptions are therefore limited to a maximum of five shillings each."[27]

The response was overwhelming and branches vied with each other for the honour and pleasure of making the presentation itself. In the event it was the Cork branch, in association with the Annual Council of the Comhaltas, which bade farewell formally to Maurice Walsh on 30 June 1934. Caroline was present too. A smoking concert was followed by a supper and many speeches. A. M. Connell, who had succeeded Humphrey Kerins as president, described Maurice Walsh as a whole man and said he had read somewhere that he was a tradition in himself. He too had that feeling that Maurice was what an officer of the service should grow up to be. J. J. Waldron, then the inspector, recalled his early association with Maurice in Comhaltas work and paid tribute to him and to Caroline. He said that Peter O'Donovan in one of his bright moments remarked that "here was a Distillery Officer married to a lady who *could* make punch, and yet they say marriages are not made in heaven – Pooh!"

It was Humphrey Kerins, fittingly, who had the last word. He dwelt on the theme of friendship in which he thought that Maurice Walsh excelled more than in any other quality. He had achieved very reat success and never lost a friend by it. Humphrey recalled someone who had lost friends through too much success being described in the terms, "The sun of prosperity fell on him and he could not stand the heat." Maurice Walsh had stood the heat and he always would.

Humphrey then went on to present Maurice with a portrait of himself in crayons by Sean O'Sullivan, R.H.A. With the portrait went a fine writing table and chairs. The portrait was exhibited that year in the Irish Royal Academy.

Maurice himself was much moved and for once spoke in low key. "From what I have heard I rather suspect that I have a lot of friends here tonight: more friends than any one man could wish for." And of course he spoke of the service in particularly affectionate terms.

I am proud of it. In that pride I cannot but feel a wistfulness that I have left the fighting ranks. It is a peculiar thing that any man I have ever worked with I held to be my colleague – in the true sense of the word – from the bottom rung to the top in this Service of ours . . . If there is anything I want to speak about here tonight it is the fellowship of men. There are grand men in the world! It makes life worth its salt to have met and known them and to have gone seeking for them . . .[28]

It was an emotional evening at the Hotel Metropole and it marked the end of an era. Maurice Walsh had left the service in which he had spent his working life and left the association that meant so much to him – or at least its "fighting ranks". He was fifty-five and at the peak of his writing power, with a growing international reputation. The decision to resign had not been an easy one but he had made it and now he was independent.

Part 3.

Distilling and Maturing.

Independence: 1934 - 1964.

Maurice Walsh in 1937.

Chapter 9. **Written Output.**

While Maurice Walsh was working at the "silent" distillery on the Liffey at Chapelizod, meeting new friends like Peter O'Donovan and Jack Spears and getting more and more involved in the work of the Comhaltas, he still managed to find time for writing, for gardening and for building himself a summerhouse at St Michael's. He was a man who needed a private place and built a summerhouse or something similar wherever he lived once he had started writing again. His press and magazine pieces (which have not yet been collected) began to increase as the number of his books and with them the demand for his work grew. Success, as always, began to breed success.

Maurice's writing career received an enormous boost when J. M. Barrie sent him an unsolicited testimonial which Chambers were then able to use on the dust covers of subsequent books. It was a handsome tribute from one of the most popular authors of the day.

Please let a fellow author tell you that he has been having some very happy hours over *The Key Above the Door*. Indeed, I could put it more strongly, for I lay a-bed, a semi-invalid, rather thrilled that such a fine yarn had come out of the heather. I felt like a discoverer, too, as I alighted on it by accident and without any anticipation of the treat that was in store. I am enamoured of your book and stop to give you three cheers.

That phrase, "out of the heather", was a telling one. It was particularly apt in relation to *The Key Above the Door* but tended to become the touchstone by which reviewers evaluated his later books and that did not work to his advantage. Some of his best stories did come out of the heather of Scotland and Ireland, but by no means all of them.

After the Barrie tribute became public knowledge sales of Maurice's books began to grow steadily. *The Key* itself sold hugely but without additional financial benefit to Maurice himself as he had sold that story outright to Chambers for the *Journal*. His second book, *While Rivers Run*, appeared in 1928 and sold 5,540 copies in the United Kingdom and Ireland in that first year, 14,137 in 1929 and 13,888 in 1930. *The Small Dark Man* came out in October 1929 and sold 11,670 before the end of that year and 26,393 in 1930. Both appeared in serial form in *Chambers Journal* first. By 1929 Maurice's books were also appearing in America. They were handled through the publishing agencies of Brandt and Brandt and Lipincott and appeared both in magazines and book form, published by Fred A. Stokes.

After *The Small Dark Man* was published Maurice had an irate letter from an English clergyman complaining about the number of times the words "bloody" and "damn" had been used. He had counted them. Maurice was delighted. He enjoyed writing that book and particularly composing the little verses that head each chapter. Maurice Walsh the poet has been sadly neglected and more about that will be said in Chapter 13. However, the individual verses in the book *The Small Dark Man* were early essays in that art and, in keeping with the vigorous but romantic nature of the book, were by turns wistful and energetic. Maurice himself found it hard to stay serious even when he thought something serious was called for. Chapter XVII of the book deals with the climactic big fight – and a marvellously effective fight it is. The action has clearly been leading up to it for some time even though the hero Hugh Forbes has been trying to keep the peace. The verse at the head of that chapter reads:

Out of the brute
Have we evolved,
To rule by mind have we resolved,
But if you want to sooth your woes
Go meet your foe and blood his nose.

There is a family story of Maurice sitting by the fireside in St Michael's swiftly composing the verses for *The Small Dark Man* and reaching this one. There is a pause while he looks into the fire and the family quietly continue with whatever each member is doing. Maurice looks up and glances at his wife and sons with a twinkle in his eye, then suddenly cries:

Hit him again while you're able
Or else he'll hit ye in the navel.

At this time, Maurice was also working on a collection of shorter stories to be linked by a connection with Hugh Forbes, the Small Dark Man, as leader of a flying column during the Black and Tan war. The genesis of that series lay in the first book when Forbes and his friend Tearlath are talking about their experiences in the First World War. Forbes goes on to talk of seven years of fighting and is pulled up by the villain.

"Four, was it not?" put in Stark.
"Oh that war! Any real fighting I saw came after that."
"In Ireland? Were you what is called a Black-and-Tan?"
"I would rather be the devil." There was warm conviction in the deep tones.[29]

The first story in the linked collection that was to be called *Green Rushes* appeared in 1930 in the Christmas issue of *Chambers Journal*. It was called "Over the Border". That year also saw a short article for the *SMT Magazine* called "The Mountain Lands of Badenoch" which had been called for by Neil Gunn, who produced a companion piece. Maurice himself was extremely busy at this time with the work of his staff association. He was president of the Comhaltas in 1929-30.

No more written work appeared until 1932 but his fourth book turned out to be one of his best. He had been working on it intermittently ever since the first version was serialised in the *Irish Emerald* in 1908. *Blackcock's Feather* owes its story to the early work but is inestimably better written and characterised. Maurice Walsh's accomplishments (and defects) as a storyteller are discussed in Chapter 13, but *Blackcock's Feather* is such an appealing historical novel that its first mention in this book cannot be passed over without a further glimpse of its magic. Take just the start and listen to the cunning storyteller that Maurice Walsh had become setting the scene deftly in his first two sentences.

> This is the story of me, David Gordon, and I will begin it on that day in May that I walked down the quay-wall at mouth of Avon, below Bristol, and held discourse with one Diggory, sailing-master of the Speckled Hind. I begin it on that day because it was on that day Life began for me.

Surely no one could resist reading on after such a start?

Blackcock's Feather appeared in *Chambers Journal* first, beginning in January 1932, and was published in book form in July. It sold 14,079 copies before the end of the year. The high quality of its English prose was recognised immediately and in 1933 a text book edition was brought out by Browne and Nolan for use in Irish schools. The authorities struck out as unsuitable for children some of the finest passages, such as the glorious sword song of Gillian the Black and the love song of Bright Una. These are still unhappily missing from the edition being used in schools today but the compliment to Maurice Walsh the writer remains valid for all that. In 1937 the Department of Education authorised an Irish version, *Cleite Clarcollig*, translated by D. O'Kelly of Browne and Nolan.

Maurice's reputation back in Kerry was already high but this fourth book was received with rapture. Bryan MacMahon, that generous mine of information on all things pertaining to Listowel and North Kerry, including Maurice Walsh, remembers meeting Maurice on one of his trips back to Kerry at that time going into Spillane's shop in Listowel, which was not far from Dan Flavin's bookshop where *Blackcock's Feather* was set out in bold display in the window. Maurice was wearing a blackcock's feather in his own hat and Bryan suggested that it should be adopted as the name and emblem of the local Gaelic football team. Maurice was deeply touched and readily agreed. He had a set of jerseys made for the team, each with a blackcock's feather on the breast.

Dan Flavin was a famous Listowel character who really needs the tongue of Bryan MacMahon to make him live again. His brother Mick is still talked about in Listowel as a turbulent nationalist M.P. at Westminster who once threw the mace on the floor of the House of Commons, Dan Flavin was passionately interested in books and read everything. He had a busy flour and meal shop in Listowel but his passion got the better of him and he turned it into a bookshop during the renaissance of interest in literature and letters that flowered in Ireland during the early part of the century. The Black and Tans burned him out but he used the compensation he secured after the peace to bring in the biggest stock of books in Ireland seen outside Dublin, including the whole of the Everyman Library. Bryan MacMahon remembers being shown one of twenty-four copies of the first edition of *Ulysses* that Dan imported direct from Paris. He also recalls Dan's introducing a scheme under which anyone who bought a book for seven shillings and sixpence and kept it clean could exchange it with sixpence for any book in the shop. Sean O'Faolain said of Danny that if he had a good book he could not bear to part with it and if he had a poor book he could not bear to sell it. He was a man of great enthusiasm for books and naturally made much of local authors.

The year 1932 then was a significant one for Walsh the writer but it was a sad one for the man and his wife. Caroline had not been in good health since 1929 but in 1932 she had a late baby, a daughter christened Elizabeth, who died after three months. It had been a difficult confinement and Caroline, with a badly enlarged heart, never really recovered. She was bedridden from time to time, though not prevented completely from getting about. Trips back to Scotland became much more of an effort. Maurice was very considerate but occasionally put his foot in it without thinking. In 1933 he was writing to Scotland:

> Toshon is not speaking to me since Sunday night, when I insulted all her friends. I didn't either, but she thought I did, which is the same thing.[30]

However, 1933 ended with a success, in fact with a major break-through, with the first sale of a Maurice Walsh story to the *Saturday*

Evening Post, a lucrative market. That was the story to be the best known of all in the *Green Rushes* collection, "The Quiet Man", with very fine illustrations by F. R. Gruger. The *Saturday Evening Post* was to make a particularly good job of illustrating Maurice's stories with one notable exception "The Bonesetter" when they got the period wholly wrong. Sale of "The Quiet Man" brought in $2,000 from the *Post* and the story appeared in the issue of 11 February 1933. Nearly twenty years later John Ford was to turn it into a memorable film. Shawn Kelvin, as the hero is called in the original story, is "a blithe young lad of twenty, [who] went to the States to seek his fortune". On his return he finds that the family land has been absorbed, in an underhanded and mean way, into the "ranch" of Big Liam O'Grady of Moyvalla. In the version published in *Green Rushes* in 1935 the names were changed to Paddy Bawn Enright and Red Will Danaher. Some other details were also changed, but that word "ranch" for the Moyvalla farm remained. It obviously had some appeal for a predominantly American audience like the readers of the *Saturday Evening Post* but in fact its significance is much deeper than that because "ranch" in Ireland had been used as a term of abuse for a large estate from which the tenants had been evicted since before Land League days.

Publication of a story in the *Saturday Evening Post* was a major landmark in Maurice Walsh's career as a writer. The magazine paid very well and the stories could then be published in book form in the States, the United Kingdom and elsewhere. That was the arrangement he was to follow thereafter, as far as possible. Brandt and Brandt tried to place his work in the States first, with Chambers continuing to publish in the UK.

The American connection began through Walsh relatives in New York, the Kissanes, one of whom worked for Brandt and Brandt. Carl Brandt, who was to become a friend, placed Maurice's stories in the United States wherever he could. His brother Erd Brandt was an assistant editor at the *Saturday Evening Post* and he accepted "The Quiet Man". Carl did a lot of editing of Maurice's stories to cut them down to the *Post's* preferred length but the changes were not always to Maurice's satisfaction. Brandt reported to Maurice that Costain of the *Post* had told him, through Erd, that "if you would only tone down the sentimental atmosphere and build up your story values, there is no doubt in his mind that you would write many things for them."[31]

Maurice discussed that with Neil Gunn who very properly and sensibly told him to forget the Brandt and Brandt advice and write for himself on subjects of his own choosing, which he did. The wrangles over text went on but the Brandt connection was a profitable one for a man who had been earning £450 per annum in 1933, the maximum of the officer grade. In 1935, for example, he earned $6,115.95 net through Brandt and Brandt. In 1935 and 1936, American editions of *The Road to Nowhere* and *Green Rushes* alone sold over 18,000 copies.

Another memorable event in 1933 was the formation of "The Ancient and Honourable Society of Walshians" in Montana by a group headed by the noted writer of American western stories Eugene Manlove Rhodes and including four of his close friends, F. R. Burnham, J. J. McBride, J. R. O'Neil and Philip E. Kubrick. These western American admirers of Maurice Walsh wrote the "constitution" of their society inside the cover of *While Rivers Run* and sent Maurice a photograph of it.

> We do formally believe that Maurice Walsh is in the line of apostolic succession, belonging to the glorious company headed by R. L. S. and Barrie, companion to Martin.
> Purpose: to call attention of denizens of these non United, as it were, States to the fact that a great man walks the common ways of earth. [32]

Maurice Walsh himself was delighted and flattered but with typical modesty much embarrassed by the comparison with other writers. He was a great admirer of Eugene Manlove Rhodes and became very friendly with him and his wife Mary. He paid tribute to Rhodes in several of his books, particularly *The Hill Is Mine*, which came out shortly after Eugene Manlove Rhodes died.

> He had the sun in his books — sun and mountain and plain and desert, and the colours o' them. And his men were bonny men and trusty — honest by choice, betimes, and not by necessity. Homesick he used to make me.
> He was homesick himself, exiled twenty years from his New Mexico. I knew him — a good man to take along, small, virile and great hearted. [33]

They shared the same fundamental beliefs in good and trusty male fellowship. Eugene Manlove Rhodes writing about the tight comradeship of men of the range, "working for the brand" and counting and relying on each other's steadfastness and honour, was quarrying the same ground that for Maurice Walsh produced the fraternity of Loch Ruighi in the books and Lochindorb in life, people who were sib to each other and to the high ideals of an ancient place and nation. The two men were brothers under the skin and the pen and were quick to recognise each other. They met when Maurice was in America in 1938 as the president of Irish PEN; Eugene died soon after.

By the end of 1933 Maurice had resigned from the Excise Service on a pension of £376 per annum, supplemented by considerable earnings from his writings. His books were selling steadily both at home and abroad. Certainly he was successful enough to contemplate a move from St Michael's and in 1934 he bought Ard na Glaise (the height of the little stream) at Blackrock on the other side of Dublin. It was a big house with about three acres of ground around it, backing on to a convent estate. Caroline loved it as soon as she set eyes on it. Maurice was reluctant to commit himself since he thought that the price (£1,400) was too high. When they went to see it finally together with the agent he said gruffly, "I don't like it."

Caroline burst into tears and he immediately said, "Okay, we'll take it."

They moved in right away and Thomasheen James moved with them.

Thomasheen James O'Doran, the subject of sixteen of Maurice Walsh's stories, his man-of-no-work, was not entirely the product of his vivid imagination but in fact a sort of family hanger-on who became an institution and whose real name was Tom O'Gorman. In the late 1920's when Maurice was building his summerhouse at St Michael's Tom simply walked into his life and stayed.

> I first made his acquaintance through the medium of a claw hammer. I was amateurishly putting a new roof on my summerhouse at the garden-foot and the hammer, after the way of hammers, slid away from my fingers and disappeared over the eaves. A startled "Wow" accompanied by a sacred epithet came up from below, and I nearly followed the hammer as I craned over the edge.
>
> I was looking down on Thomasheen James.
>
> A live, wary, china-blue eye was contemplating me from each side of a sharp peeled nose standing out of a freckled face.[34]

Thus entered Tom O'Gorman. Maurice Walsh had always a soft spot for underdogs and lame dogs, hobos and itinerants of all kinds, for "the broken men" who wandered the roads, especially if they had a ready tongue and the cheek of the devil. This one simply made himself at home.

Tom O'Gorman had been on the roads intermittently all his life, living from pillar to post. Maurice was about fifty at this time and Tom would have been a few years younger, so far as anyone could tell. He came originally from Arklow but when he was a small child his mother was caught trying to steal a pair of shoes and he was taken from her and put into an orphanage. He had a varied life when he left the orphanage. He joined the British navy for a time and his ship took

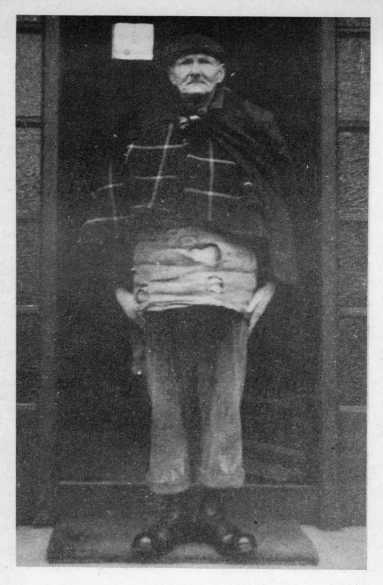

Thomasheen James

part in the evacuation of the White Russians from Archangel during the First World War. Back in Ireland he made his base in and around Dublin, though with frequent wanderings away in the country, and did odd jobs for people, Maurice Walsh included, sleeping in the garden shed at St Michael's whenever he felt inclined. When the Walsh family moved from St Michael's to Ard na Glaise, Thomasheen moved his few belongings and the lawnmower in a wheelbarrow, staying overnight in Dublin with one of his cronies – the Dublin "jackeen" Davy Hand of the stories.

Thomasheen James on paper was a brighter and more attractive character than the real life Thomasheen O'Gorman but there was certainly a bond between him and "the boss", who felt a good deal of wry affection and responsibility for the wayward and unreliable Tom. He got the more erratic as he grew older and was a weird figure to see (Maurice dubbed him "The evolution of homo sapiens: the final result"), so weird in fact that he could not realistically be described in the stories about Thomasheen James as he really was.

> He might be thirty. He might even be fifty. He had a lean, blonde, unwrinkled, bony face with nut-cracker jaws, and his prominent eyes were light-blue and brilliant as a northern sea in summer. An old tweed hat, with the rim stagged off, rested like a fez on bat-wing ears. Instead of an overcoat he wore a fragment of a red-and-green plaid over his shoulders and round his hips, not unlike a kilt, was a bleached flour-sack. His blue dungaree pants stopped half-way down his lean shanks, and his immense boots still showed traces of a brilliant morning polish. He was just sane enough to be eccentric and, sometimes, cunningly wise, and forever subject to changes of mood from minute to minute.[35]

That was the real Tom in later years, though it describes another fictional character in a Maurice Walsh book.

Thomasheen James the fictional character appeared first in the *Saturday Evening Post* in December 1935 in a story called "Thirty Pieces of Copper" and that came about as a result of two quite different influences. The first was that the story itself was based on a true incident when the irrepressible Tom, left alone and without funds when Maurice and Toshon had gone to Kerry over a holiday period, pawned a pair of Maurice's waders to keep himself going until "the boss" returned. The point of the incident (and the story) was that Maurice trusted Thomasheen, suspected him of betraying the trust and yet was himself at fault because he had, as Thomasheen reasoned, intended to leave him some money before he left for Kerry but forgot. They never had a formal employer and employee relationship but funds were provided when needed. There was always food, even when the Walshes were away, but it was some money Tom needed. In the complex responsibilities that Maurice imposed on himself, he found himself feeling quite a bit guilty over this incident.

The second influence that went to the making of the Thomasheen James character was that of Neil Gunn, since the incident occurred just about the time that Neil was pressing Maurice to take the initiative with Brandt and the *Saturday Evening Post* on the question of the kind of stories he should write and how he should structure them.

> This business of trying to think out a single short story is not enough for you in your attained position. It is too much of a struggle in the void and in itself does not tend automatically to produce others. You want a background and a set of individuals that would be a sort of breeding ground in the vague way that your Small Dark Man and company did become. Very well, I suggest Dublin and a new set of characters. Once you have got them lodged in your mind I *know* that they would go on doing things until I'd have to use physical force to stop you and them! You hate the thought of that just now. It's like a great mountain that you'd have to sweat blood to move. But *whatever* is suggested would be like that. You know all this just as well as I do. What you really want to do is to shirk it. I know you to your last lazy atom – knowing a little of myself![36]

Neil Gunn suggested stories written in the first person, about a young, adventurous American in Dublin "who in a series of adventures – each a complete short story in itself – would penetrate all sections of its life – social, governmental, artistic etc. in a way that would be realistic and romantic." The plan Neil suggested was that if the *Saturday Evening Post* favoured such an idea Neil would provide the plots and Maurice would write them up and they would share the spoils. They had done so before. Neil had helped a lot with *While Rivers Run* but this was to be a much bigger undertaking. "I know it sounds big," wrote Neil, "but the bigger the better and be damned. Together we are capable of any iniquity . . . Think of me signing an agreement to write forty thousand words on whisky! That should give you courage. You couldn't write worse than I have done."

It was a good idea. Neil was quick at thinking up plots and Maurice's storytelling style was in great demand. Maurice himself was not keen on using an American as his central character, however, simply because he did not have enough experience of and feel for Americans at that early stage in his career. He was to make up for it later. What Maurice did produce was the first Thomasheen James story, which was just what the *Post* wanted. So much for the inception of Thomasheen James. Out of such a complex of circumstances and influences comes a brand new literary character.

At Ard na Glaise, Tom O'Gorman settled down in the stables and made himself comfortable. Maurice settled down in the new summerhouse to write more stories and articles and to produce a new book every two years or so. He began to have trouble with his wrist about this time and ever after needed to wear a leather strap on it as it became swollen when he was writing. He was still writing in pencil in old Excise ledger books, occasionally drawing horses' heads in the margins while he was searching for the right phrase or twist in the story. He liked to write in the mornings so far as possible and leave the afternoons free for gardening or some other activity.

Maurice was always a very keen and industrious gardener and had plenty of scope at Ard na Glaise, with or without the help of Thomasheen. He had a great fund of personally observed garden lore that he would pass on to his friends, if they would listen.

Lettuce grown under glass is poisonous stuff. Lettuce should not be eaten until June. Before that, it causes indigestion and belchings and the worship of Aphrodite – same as tomatoes.[37]

If he found himself stumped in a story he liked to go out into the garden for a bit. He would pick up a hoe or a rake and just poke about with it, pretty aimlessly, until the right word or phrase came to him, when he would drop the tool and dash off back into the summerhouse to get on with the real work. Alternatively he would go and ask Toshon or the maid (for they could afford a maid by this time) if green went with red in a woman's costume, anything to break the deadlock and start the words flowing again. Not that he was often stuck, for all that he could poke fun at himself and at his own tested stock situation "out of the heather". "My red-haired heroine said that she preferred the blond Nordic villain to the squat black Celtic hero. So did I."[38]

Once when he had been stuck for some time he came home from Boland's pub with fresh ideas and wrote far into the night. In the morning, though, he tore it all up. "Too hectic," he said simply.

The year 1934 saw publication of the fifth book, *The Road to Nowhere*, a cleverly constructed story about an educated man living and travelling for a time with a small band of tinkers – itinerants. The two main tinker characters, Jamesey Coffey, king of the road, and Maag Carty, were based on real people he had known in Kerry in his boyhood: strong, dark, good looking people who were always welcome at Ballydonoghue and who used to sit for hours exchanging news and gossip and stories with John Walsh. The book caused a considerable outcry amongst the establishment in Ireland which thought that the "itinerant" problem should be recognised as a serious matter of social concern and not idealised in that way. Maurice was unabashed and indeed went on encouraging itinerants. They would call at his home, sure of a bite and sup and a few shillings besides, or would touch him for something at the races in Listowel or elsewhere. They kept coming to his home even after he moved from Ard na Glaise in 1950 and continued coming right up to his death and beyond it. A photograph of Maurice with Pádraic Ó Conaire, a well known itinerant writer, and his ass on O'Connell Street Bridge appeared in the paper, with a further round of discussions on the radio and in the press. And the book was a success through it all, at home and abroad.

Maurice himself did not give a fig for the disapproval of the establishment, which he was to incur later in several other ways. He remembered the fine travelling people he had known as a boy and the remnants of the broken, wandering clans he had encountered in Scotland and saw no reason in the severe atmosphere of de Valera's Free State to doubt that travelling people were still well worth knowing. If they touched him for a few shillings, what harm? He could write another story about them and sell it to the *Saturday Evening Post* or even to a different magazine. A Dutch edition of *The Road to Nowhere* came out even before the end of 1934.

That year 1934 in fact saw the second Maurice Walsh story in the *Saturday Evening Post*, still part of the Quiet Man collection. It was "Then Came the Captain's Daughter", which incorporated the lyrical tale of the flight of the Colleen Oge, little Ellen Molouney, from her hard uncle and her rescue by the kindly, reassuring ghost of her dead father.

Time was moving on. Maurice was fifty-seven in 1936 when his father John Walsh died at the age of eighty-six. Ever since the death of his wife Elizabeth in 1913 he had lived on at Ballydonoghue, seeing to the farm (though it was really run by his brother Paddy with the help of Paddy Bawn), reading widely and drinking pints. He slept in the Men's Room then in one of the two double beds there and always said his prayers on his knees in the mornings. His son Maurice had published six books by the time John died and dedicated one of them to him to his great pride and satisfaction.

Maurice himself was not a slave to the pen. At the rate of a book every two years or so he left himself plenty of time for socialising. Friends always meant a good deal to him and once he made them he stayed close to them. Saturday night in those days and after was Excise night at Ard na Glaise. The coterie at Blackrock included Jim Flood, who had been governor of Athlone prison during the Troubles, Eugene O'Connor, Peter O'Donovan, Humphrey Kerins and Tom

Mongey. Tom used to read the complete works of Shakespeare every year. He was a hoplologist, a collector of swords and similar weapons, and under his influence Maurice collected a few swords and an assegai. It was Tom's hobby that promoted the title of the story "The Hoplologist" which was originally called "The Sword of Yung-lo" and which first appeared in *Chambers Journal* in 1952.

Maurice was often out and about in Dublin or down to Kerry or back to Scotland visiting friends. Sometimes Caroline was with him and sometimes not, depending on her health. It was Caroline who drove the family car though, with a great deal of pleasure if an uncertain sense of direction. She was always getting lost and taking the wrong road but when finally convinced of that she would simply say, "Ah, but it's a bonnie wee roadie."

When Caroline was very ill in 1940, Neil Gunn wrote to Maurice to ask for her and said that, in spite of his trepidation, he hoped she would soon be bowling into Dublin once again.

She bowled pretty well and consistently while the going was good. Once or twice to me it was a fair substitute for big-game hunting in Africa and I never failed to admire the way you cowered and endured with a fortitude that saw every approaching car within ten miles and was never voiceless. Begod, we were game. But at our best, our sangfroid, our nonchalance, was a pale affair beside the full-blooded, darlin' gaiety of the girl herself. Wagner should have seen her before he did his stuff about the Valkyries – or whatever.[39]

Maurice never learned to drive. None of his crowd did except for Peter O'Donovan, and that did not last. Humphrey Kerins had a friend who bought a second-hand car and called for Humphrey to take him for an admiring spin. After a bit the car began to falter and then stopped altogether. Both men got out and looked at it, neither knowing the first thing about the internal combustion engine. They opened the bonnet and looked in and shut it again, none the wiser. They walked all round the car and contemplated it and noticed a wet trail behind it, running away up the road. They followed it for a bit but it showed no signs of drying up. Water? Had the car boiled over? What should you do if it had? It was a puzzle and in the way of quiet, contemplative men Humphrey scratched his head and took out his pipe to aid concentration with a smoke. And dropped the match unthinkingly. The resultant inferno was the talk of Dublin for days.

One night Maurice and several other friends were at the house of Eugene O'Connor (who did not drive either) quite late, when the son of Charles Kennedy called at Ard na Glaise looking for his father on the instructions of his irate mother who had been waiting for him for hours. Caroline was in bed but got up, put a coat over her nightie, got

Toshon's car.

the car out and drove with the boy the short distance to Eugene
O'Connor's house. There were five round the kitchen table in a haze
of pipe smoke but with their minds illuminated in the brilliant,
blinding light of reason that a few drams of good whiskey brings. Poor
Charles Kennedy got told off for neglecting his family and the others
slipped away sheepishly before Caroline's coated and nightied stern
figure.

Maurice was not drunk though, in his own phrase, he had drink
taken, quite a lot of drink taken. Feeling a bit guilty about forgetting
the time, he wanted to appear sober and when they got into the car he
gave careful instructions to his wife. "Turn left here, Toshon. Change
gear now," and so on. It was only a few streets back to Ard na Glaise
but he was so serious and dignified about his instructions that Caroline
had to laugh, as he knew she would.

By the late 1930s Maurice was a well known figure and Ireland's
best selling novelist. Magazines like *The Field* and the *Irish Tatler* were
soliciting pieces from him instead of his submitting them for approval
or rejection. He had written some good books, some amusing stories
and better poetry than anyone realised. In 1937 there appeared the
book he himself regarded as his best, *And No Quarter*, which presented
"the chronicles of the wars of Montrose as seen by Martin Somers,
Adjutant of Women in O'Cahan's Regiment". It is dedicated to Seán
Ó Hógain "in token of the historical and Gaelic scholarship placed so
generously at my disposal". Seán was a good friend and a frequent
visitor to the Walsh home, where he used to play chess with Maurice's
eldest son Maurice. Maurice the author never learned to play chess
and knew only a little about the game but he used to watch for a bit
until the going got difficult and the two players grew quiet with
concentration. When no moves had been made for a bit, Maurice
used to lean over to his son and say, "Why don't you check him?"
Seán used to go through the roof.

The book is a stunning tale, discussed further in Chapter 13.
Maurice was proud of it but sent it to Chambers with some reticence
since it was very different from the books that had gone before.

Here is that long promised yarn, that small egg or mouse or
whatever you care. I have sent a copy to Brandt who may send it to
the *Saturday Evening Post*. The *Post* will not accept it probably, very
probably as it is not in their style. If they do not, no doubt Brandt
will try otherwheres but I have told him that Chambers would then
be free (after refusal by *Post*) to consider whether it was worth
serialisation in the *Journal*. Anyway, I am sending it to you to look it
over and vet it. You will note that I tried to write it from a new
angle, the Gaelic angle, the plain soldier's angle. I think it is too

leisurely in the beginning. An old man is supposed to be telling the yarn. He would be too leisurely and discursive. I don't know what you experts . . . will be thinking of it and its historical reconstruction. My principal authorities are Buchan, the Black Book of Clan Ranald (It's in Gaelic and difficult Gaelic), the Ormonde papers, Bain's "History of Nairnshire" and Ritchie's "Pageant of Morayland". However, you will tell me frankly, as usual.[40]

The original title had been the full Covenating cry of *Jesus, and No Quarter* but Toshon was a bit scandalised at that and Chambers were not too keen on it either – or on the harsh things said about the Covenanters. We shall return to that at a later stage. However, Maurice had as usual discussed his work with Neil Gunn while he was writing it and Neil had given him both encouragement and a characteristic Gunn warning.

> You'll be hearing from your pal Carl about *And No Quarter*. Good news it'll be, whatever it is. It'll be your best book besides. The only respect in which you are like poetry and wine is in the slow, inevitable, cumulative certainty of the maturing process. I'm longing to see the thing in print. I'll look for a certain quality which may not be there. If it isn't, I'll tell you with great frankness. That it'll be moving in many parts I have no doubt. That's not what I mean. But you are becoming an artist, there's no doubt, also a moneymongerer on a large scale. The two sides do now and then have a friendly tussle. But I offer no comment. How can I, who am glad to get £2-2-0 for an article and it well thought out and carefully written?[41]

Neil's own *Highland River* was due out on 1 April that year although he was very modest about it, as indeed he was the following year about winning the James Tait Black prize for it. His reaction to seeing *And No Quarter* in print when it came out later in 1937 must have warmed Maurice Walsh's heart: "I read it all in one long dithering wallop and me in bed recovering from a temperature and Daisy beside me with one growing."

He thought it had its faults:

> . . . being slow, maybe, in the beginning as they say, with expressions of romance at long odd moments that my thin bloodedness might not have courage for, and so on and what not here and there, but what do they all amount to but the just personal mannerisms of the traditional storyteller? . . . Tippermuir got me where I thought there was nothing of me left and it moved me, by God, like the war pipes. Cheers to you, boy! The atmosphere of that Gaelic camp is thick with easy life. And if you give the Covenant folk hell, they

deserved most of it.[42]

Maurice was right about the *Saturday Evening Post*. They did not like the new book at all and commented that "the story itself was so overshadowed by the propaganda that it lost out entirely". God knows what "propaganda" meant there. Historical detail, probably. At any event it was too rich for the *Post's* blood so Brandt sold it to *Adventure* magazine for $1,200, and thought he had done well. However, Howard Bloomfield, the editor of *Adventure*, was furious to find that he had to pay Chambers £75 for serial rights to permit UK circulation on account of exporting the magazine to England. There was quite a lot of acrimonious correspondence into which Maurice was dragged, though it was little to do with him. It upset him quite a lot, though, and Neil Gunn had to tell him firmly to keep out of it and let the publishers and agents sort it out for themselves. Neil was a great strength in these things. The two families were close and met often and Maurice relied on him heavily for business advice as well as for the occasional plot for a story. Both were involved in their respective branches of PEN, the writers' organisation, discussed in more detail in Chapter 12.

The year 1938 produced another fine work, *Sons of the Swordmaker*, based on his old story of "The Woman Without Mercy" and the ancient tale of the sacking of the hostel of Da Derga, all skilfully blended together and lyrically told, but it was an unconventional book for the time and did not prove popular. One interesting fact about it is that the Talbot Press wrote to Chambers in 1938 suggesting that for personal and national reasons Maurice Walsh was anxious to have at least one of his books produced in Ireland and that they wanted to bring out the specifically Irish tale on which he was working – then to be called *The Hostel of Da Derga*. That was fine but it quickly was followed by a strong rumour that Maurice was to publish all his subsequent books in Ireland. Chambers checked with him and quickly issued a denial in the *Bookseller and Publishing Circular*. Maurice was by then a very important author in any publisher's list.

During that same year, 1938, Maurice and Caroline and their son Ian spent a pleasant week on the Thurso River with Neil and Daisy Gunn and Neil's brother Alec. The fishing on that beat was normally very expensive but the keeper was an old friend. Maurice never caught a fish the whole week but enjoyed himself hugely. Ian brought a mouth organ with him and fascinated Neil Gunn by playing "Jesu, Joy of Man's Desiring" on it in the evenings.

Ian was in practice as a doctor and the first salmon of the few they did catch that week was wrapped in leaves and sent off to his partner in Hull. Ian had married a girl called Maura, whose physical appearance his father used for the Dark Rose in *And No Quarter*, but she died in 1937 giving birth to their son and Maurice and Caroline's first grandson, also called Maurice. It is a curious fact of family history that Caroline's sister Bertha, who married Maurice's friend in the Excise Percy Knight, died when their son Colin was born. Maurice went to stay with Percy, who was distraught at the time and remained with him until he was sufficiently recovered from the shock. When Ian lost his wife, Percy's son Colin came to stay with him to fill a similar role. The Walsh friendships were and are like that.

By 1938, the year of Munich, the shadows were already lengthening and when Ian decided to join the Royal Army Medical Corps towards the end of that year, Maurice and Caroline decided that England was no place for their grandson and took him back to Ireland with them. Caroline was increasingly bedridden but used to read Dickens to the little boy and threaten him with a black hairbrush if he got into mischief. Sometimes she had to use it!

The outbreak of war put an end to trips back to Scotland and to visits from Scottish friends and relatives, though correspondence continued, the censor permitting. Life in neutral Ireland went on and Maurice continued to write stories for the *Saturday Evening Post*. That magazine was soon asking for Thomasheen James to entertain the American troops in Northern Ireland once America came into the war, but Maurice did not care to take his popular character to Belfast. He felt it would not fit in with the strict line he followed on Irish neutrality.

Tom O'Gorman was still around, though. In 1941 Maurice sent him on an errand to his friend Humphrey Kerins, ten miles away, giving him five bob for subsistence.

Humphrey gave him a glass of whiskey, which is fatal . . . Thomasheen went on from there, consumed the crown in the shape of six pints of plain and had to walk from town, high, wide and handsome and the road was not wide enough . . . Usually, he is moderate in drink but when he is immoderate, let the democracies take shelter. He comes round to me to express his views on "Ingland" that he once fought for and I gather that her disasters are due to his absence from the fray – but of course many Irishmen hold similar views, poor fellows . . . He wonders "What'n hell that paper shark Max Aitken is doin' out o' Canada?" I didn't know who Max was till he told me.[43]

The war years saw the publication of several stories and four books, although increasing shortage of paper in the UK made production there difficult. The four books were *The Hill Is Mine* (1940), *Thomasheen James, Man-of-no-Work* (1941), *The Spanish Lady* (1943) and *The Man in*

Brown (1945), which was Maurice's first detective story, written in collaboration with a journalist and playwright called David Sears. The book is dedicated to him with characteristic warmth and generosity. A Talking Book version of *Thomasheen James* for use by the blind also came out in 1941.

That year brought a savage hurt, however, with the death of Toshon on 10 January. She had not been well for many years, particularly since the birth and death of Elizabeth in 1932, and as the years went by she got steadily more frail in body, if not in spirit. Happily, she was able to accompany Maurice on his trip to America in 1938 as the president of Irish PEN, but the visit took a lot out of her. Her last year was not an easy one.

> What I want to tell you most emphatically is that the best thing has happened for Toshon. You remember that in 1929 she was in a bad way and we did not expect her to be anything but an invalid for the rest of her days. Yet, as she said herself, thereafter she had the best eleven years of her life. She was gallant hearted and my ideal was that she die debonairly on her feet. That was not to be . . . Even under heroin and luminol she never went deep under and was able to tell us all she would like us to do, was sorry for us but happy in herself.[44]

Of course life had to go on but Maurice was bitter about the suffering of that last year and showed it. For a time he stopped observing the forms of the Catholic religion and refused to go to mass. He was reconciled to the church later but was to break (and return) again. ("I've been a knave twice," he used to say.) It was from this time, too, that he began to avoid going to friends' funerals if he could. Death depressed him in any form, but particularly he felt deeply the death of a close friend and would take no solace for it. Death began to appear to him as a kind of hypocrisy, and hypocrisy he hated always.

What kept him going after Caroline died was his family, his love for them and his pride in them. It meant a great deal to him to have his family nearby. His firstborn Maurice was only three miles away. Neil, the youngest, was still at medical school. Ian was away, waiting for an overseas posting, but his son Mauricin was living with his grandfather, a lovable child with something of Toshon alive in him every day about the house.

> He is digging with his "super spade" and can he dig? I'll tell the world. His method is exactly mine, and the way he sets his foot on the tread would make you laugh. He really is a good lad . . . He is after telling me that "that bloody cat is following me everywhere".

Maurice with his grandson, Maurice (1945)

That's Thomasheen James.[45]

The Walshes were a close family and at a time like that it told. Ian went off to the Middle East and his father worried a lot about him, though he was proud as Lucifer of him, and urged all his friends and relatives to write to him "care of the Middle East Forces" as often as possible. His other two sons kept close and his old friends rallied round him with affectionate attention.

> We see Maurice Junior regularly. He has a nice house at Dun Laoghaire and two fine sons . . . He has a pleasant method of argument after one small drink – he is temperate – and has a dismissing gesture of the hand that makes Peter O'Donovan speechless, but not for long. Peter and Ethel come over often, but neither of them is too hale in body. Jack Spears comes often too, but poor Lily doesn't like to come too often – hurts too much. Neil is in a quartet today at the Feis Ceoil (the music festival, you know). He does love music and seems to know as much about it as Mr. J. B. Bach. His medical exams come easy to him, and he is now in his final stretch, but because of his age he can't qualify till near end of '42. A cool customer and his da is an old fogey. He was astounded the other day when he found that I could ride a bicycle. Gawd! All the weary miles I rode! His nephew, young Maurice, loves and respects him and will eat even porridge under his eye. Gosh we had three good sons.[46]

Neil set several of his father's songs to music, in particular "To Cashel I Am Going", "Had I the Choice of all the Queenly Ones that ever Troubled Man" from *The Key Above the Door*, "The Wandering Men of Baravais" from *Sons of the Swordmaker*, the "Sword Song of Gillian the Black" from *Blackcock's Feather* and "Finn, Cuchulain and Conal" from *The Small Dark Man*. The last is a fine sonorous piece and when Maurice heard it sung by Neil's wife Máirín he smiled and commented, "That's a man's song!"

There was never any woman in Maurice's life but Caroline – Toshon, first and last. From the beginning he was "entangled in the meshes of her long red hair" and it never dimmed for him, even long after the red had faded. Life went on after her death but there was never quite the same keen zest in him afterwards as there had been before. He remained a warm, friendly, steadfast man but the shadows touched him then as they had not done since little Molly died, and it showed. He was getting older and weaker (he was sixty-two) and so were his friends. Peter O'Donovan, he remarked, could run his temperature up and down 95 to 104 just by thinking about it, a lovely man who managed to be both a hypochondriac and a valetudinarian.

His books continued to sell in reasonable numbers, both in the United Kingdom and abroad, and brought in substantial royalties. For example, his statement from Chambers for the six months from January to June 1942 showed:

And No Quarter	4,478 copies sold
Blackcock's Feather	2,573 (plus 1,104 school copies and 4 Irish)
Green Rushes	3,048
The Hill Is Mine	2,911
The Road to Nowhere	2,849
The Small Dark Man	2,350
Sons of the Swordmaker	3,045
Thomasheen James	3,169
While Rivers Run	2,615

From those sales, his royalties were £1,092.14s.0d.

He was to publish eight more books between the end of the war and 1964, some of them largely collections of stories already published in magazines. The first was *Son of Apple* (1947), which had been written earlier but delayed by the paper shortage. Maurice "translitterated" that, to use his own phrase, from an old Irish folk tale translated from the Irish by Catriona Macleod of the Irish Folklore Society. She was the step-daughter of Paddy Little, the Minister for Posts and Telegraphs and a friend of Maurice. After that, there was *Castle Gillian* (1948), *Trouble in the Glen* (1950), *Son of a Tinker* (1951), *The Honest Fisherman* (1952), *A Strange Woman's Daughter* (1954), *Danger Under the Moon* (1956) and finally *The Smart Fellow*, which was published posthumously in 1964. Characteristically, Maurice Walsh was working on the proofs just before he died.

Chapter 10. **Theatre, Films, Radio, Television**

It was some time before Maurice Walsh's success as an author began to attract the makers of films and radio programmes. The first approach was from the film director John Ford who read the story "The Quiet Man" in the *Saturday Evening Post* in 1933 and set out to acquire the film rights, which he did in an agreement dated 25 February 1936.

The agreement gave Ford the exclusive rights for motion pictures, recording and broadcasting (from film) for the sum of $10. A second agreement, of the same date, provided that "as an inducing cause for . . . the sale of the said world motion picture" Maurice Walsh was to get $2,500 plus half the excess over that figure if Ford managed to sell the story to a picture company. There was then a third and final agreement, this time between Ford and Republic Pictures, dated 25 May 1951, which gave Ford (who then directed the film) $10,000 for the rights. So Maurice got in all $6,260 (10 + 2,500 + 3,750) for a story which made millions in its film version.

The film *The Quiet Man* starred John Wayne and Maureen O'Hara and was premiered in Ireland in May 1952. Maurice himself enjoyed it immensely: "The picture is just good entertainment, but the technicolour of the Connemara scene is extraordinar' fine. Moreover, Barry Fitzgerald steals the show."[47]

It was an immensely popular and successful film in Ireland, in America and elsewhere. When running in Paris it was reputed to have grossed more than the legendary *Gone With the Wind*. In Kerry, of course, its impact was electrifying. Maurice's sister Sister Gabriel was allowed out of the Listowel convent to see it, an unheard of concession in those days. Special editions of the *Green Rushes* stories came out all over the world – *L'Homme Tranquil* in France, *Der Stille Mann* in Germany and so on. There were Dutch, Danish and Swedish versions as well as Canadian, Australian and South African editions. Maurice won the 1952 Award of the American Screenwriters Guild, the fifth awarded, for the Best Written American Comedy. The story was dramatised in several forms, even as a musical. The *New York Times* of 8 and 9 August 1960 reported that Fred Herbert was making a musical based on "The Quiet Man" to be called *Donnybrook*, with Jack Cole as the choreographer and Eddie Foy Jnr as the star. It flopped. Maurice himself commented, " 'The Quiet Man' was first published in the *Saturday Evening Post* and later incorporated in *Green Rushes*. The scene was in my native Kerry. John Ford, who made the film, transferred the scene to Connemara; and now Mr Herbert brings it up to Donnybrook. Fair enough."[48] Donnybrook is an area on the outskirts of Dublin where Donnybrook Fair was once held. It is also an old term for a punch up.

That was not the end of the "Quiet Man" saga though. During the Second Listowel Writers' Week a dramatised version of the story was devised by Michael Kennelly and performed in and outside O'Sullivan's bar at Ballydonoghue and in a pub in Listowel, now named "The Quiet Man". The whole thing was televised by RTE.

In 1934 the first tentative suggestion was made for a film based on *The Road to Nowhere* to be made by Gaumont British but nothing came of that. However, that story continued to attract a lot of interest. In 1936 a Mrs Baxter Jackson, who had been Kathleen Forbes Leith, entered into negotiation with Brandt to write a full screenplay for stage or screen. She did a lot of work but despite encouragement from Maurice Walsh (backed strongly by Neil Gunn) nothing came of it. Carl Brandt was not much interested in the dramatic side.

An advertising and publishing firm called Cross Courtenay Ltd approached Maurice in May 1936 with the suggestion that he adapt one of his own stories or write a special screenplay about Cumberland, with scenes laid in various parts of the Lake District. Someone had seized on the fact that George Washington's mother was buried at Whitehaven and thought that was an obvious lead-in to the American market. Nothing came of that either, since Maurice was not in the least interested in the idea.

The year 1937 saw the first radio broadcast of one of his works. Irish Radio broadcast *Blackcock's Feather* in eleven episodes. Northern Ireland radio produced it the following year as a serial for children.

Attempts were still being made to get his work into films. British National Films purchased the rights of *The Key Above the Door* from Chambers in 1938 for £250 and ten per cent of the net receipts. They wanted Maurice to co-operate in making the film. Chambers had bought the story outright from Maurice for £100 for *Chambers Journal* although they paid him another £80 after the book started selling so well. There was no obligation to pay him anything from receipts from the film rights agreement but they gave him £75 (half the net profit from the £250) and promised him half of the receipts if the film were made. It was a handsome offer but unfortunately the war intervened and the idea was not revived. The agreement lapsed after fourteen years, in 1953, but by then tastes had changed.

In 1938, too, there was a talk about *Sons of the Swordmaker* on All India Radio but it was not very perceptive and worth mentioning here only to show how far afield the Walsh reputation was moving.

By 1939 Maurice had written a full length play called *The Golden Pheasant* and had some hopes that the Abbey Theatre in Dublin might take it, though they did not. It was put on in Tralee in 1944 but was not a success and Maurice himself did not like the performance. It was a comedy in three acts, all of which take place on the same day, 11 August, but it was brittle, thin stuff, a poaching episode mixed up with comic Guards in Slievenaree and a sinister old IRA feud. Maurice wrote it in collaboration with a man called Don Giltinan, a PEN vice-president, but his heart was never really in it. Chambers tried to arrange a London production in 1946 but were not very confident and expressed the view that the Irishness of it would need to be subordinated pretty considerably before a London theatrical manager would take it on. That did indeed prove to be the opinion of Wilson Barrett, the London manager they showed it to, and he said that it had too many different Irish accents for his company. Maurice was not surprised.

> I note what you say about *The Golden Pheasant*. Fair enough. I don't suppose anything can be done with it. It is too light and short as it stands. We (or my collaborator) might add a little menace to it, and give it another go. But I am not much interested and that's a fact.[49]

Walsh works continued to be heard on the radio. In 1939 Irish Radio wanted Maurice to broadcast a funny story. He did not want to do it himself, but suggested "Thomasheen James and the Blind Pension". In that year, too, a full scenario of *Blackcock's Feather* was prepared but that project collapsed with the war.

In 1943 Richard Hayward, the chairman of the Belfast PEN group and the author of several books on Irish travel, to two of which Maurice wrote a personal introduction, thought he might attempt a screenplay of *The Road to Nowhere* and asked Maurice to quote him a special, personal price for the rights. Maurice did not say yes or no since he could never bear to hurt anyone's feelings and that is what he thought the effect of a direct refusal would be (never thinking about the commercial implications at all), but he did not want Hayward to do it. Irish Radio broadcast the story in 1944.

In America *The Man in Brown* was broadcast on 17 June 1945 under the original American title of *Nine Strings to Your Bow* by Station WTZ, sponsored by the *Saturday Evening Post*. Maurice's fee for that was $260.

In 1946, after the failure of the play *The Golden Pheasant*, Maurice was still thinking about stage and screen as vehicles for his work, either new stuff or dramatisations of the old. He decided to have a go himself at writing a screenplay for *The Road to Nowhere*, using the title *When Half Gods Go*. That was taken from one of Emerson's poems:

Though thou love her as thyself,

As a self of purer clay,
Though her parting dim the day,
Stealing grace from all alive,
Heartily know
When half gods go,
The Gods arrive.

Maurice put a lot of work into the screenplay, creating some completely new scenes and situations which in turn grew eventually into a brand new book, *Castle Gillian*, which was to appear in 1948. Maurice himself said in the introduction to the screenplay:

> The story is based to a fair extent on the novel *The Road to Nowhere* . . . inasmuch as the principal characters and some of the scenes are lifted from that book; but the book is departed from in many places and the story develops on lines of its own. The hero is Rogan Stuart, architect (soon to become Rogue McCoy, tinker's curate); the heroine is Ailish Conroy, lady horse trainer; and the god let down from the machine (and probably the real hero) is Jamesy Coffey, King of the roads, into whose skin Barry Fitzgerald would fit as a hand in a glove. The scene is Ireland, high, wide and handsome. Let us go. [50]

Then follows a new start. Rogan Stuart, a busy architect, is immersed in a project to the discontent of his young wife. She is bored and neglected and goes sailing with the villain Butler. She and her child drown but Butler escapes. Stuart, in remorse and grief, drifts and drinks and nearly drowns. He is fished out of the river by Ailish and Jamesy and thereafter the plot is essentially that of the later book *Castle Gillian*, even to the final scene in court and the fight afterwards. It reads well and rushes along at a great pace but nothing ever came of it.

Maurice had another go at writing a play but did not think very highly of the final version and made no attempt to promote it. Some years later, though, he turned the play into a novel called *A Strange Woman's Daughter*. It is an almost Gothic tale of a young poet, Michael Dillane, who thinks he may be mad and who has an aunt, Margaret Gannon, thought by everyone to be mad, but free. There is a scene in Gorah madhouse which is particularly well drawn, especially in the characterisations of the bustling superintendent with a bee in his bonnet about the treatment of his patients, and of the patients themselves, the men who think they are Mahommed, Mitreza (the twentysix Buddah) and Jesus; but the novel itself is a stiff work, unlike Maurice Walsh's other books. The reason was spotted at once by Neil Gunn.

I once wrote a play and then like you turned it into a novel (*Second Sight*). You have kept to the form of the play – three acts, with entrances and exits and all – far more rigidly than I did. Your conversation has something of the stage speech. For full flavour, it would have to be spoken.[51]

Scottish Radio dramatised *The Key Above the Door* in 1950, adapted by J. B. Sellar as a Sunday night serial in seven parts.

The year 1952 saw the film *The Quiet Man* and on its success serious negotiations began for another film based on his work. Maurice authorised his publishers Chambers to negotiate with Republic Pictures, which had produced the first film, for "£3,500 more or less" for the film rights of *Trouble in the Glen* and Chambers tried to get £5,000 initially. They soon realised that this was not likely to be secured but there then began a three or four-sided argument in which Brandt and Brandt sought to persuade Maurice that he had been misled over the payment for the rights to "The Quiet Man" into accepting too small a figure and that the success of that film so increased his market value that he should get very much more for *Trouble in the Glen* than Chambers were seeking. Maurice cabled Chambers to formally raise the price to $15,000, or about £5,400 at the rate of exchange in force then. Chambers complied, with strong misgivings since their negotiations had indicated clearly that while the London manager was keen, his masters in Hollywood were much less so. Chambers telephoned the American company in Hollywood and got a flat refusal to $15,000 though they thought the film company might be pushed up to $12,000. Maurice stuck out for fifteen. What Brandt and Brandt were saying was that negotiations with an American film company needed an American firm and they thought they could get more.

The whole exchange left a nasty taste, with Maurice Walsh uncomfortably in the middle of some pretty hostile exchanges. In the end the attempt to get a higher fee misfired badly since Republic quoted different conversations with Maurice himself and Hayes of Republic over a drink, specifying $10,000 as the fee. Chambers had to write to ask him if that was so or not and of course Maurice did not have the first recollection of what he had or had not said or might have implied to agree to over a drink. He wanted to wash his hands of the whole affair but Chambers persisted on his behalf and in the end Maurice got £3,929 in cash and a lot of disillusionment with film rights negotiations. He hated the atmosphere of suspicion and back-biting, the charge and counter charge and the accusations and misunderstandings. After that experience he wanted nothing more to do with such bargaining.

That was a great pity, because in 1955 Emmet Dalton of Medal Films, and a good friend, wanted to make a film of *Blackcock's Feather* and went to the length of having a screenplay overview prepared by a man called Cecil Maiden. Maiden was enthusiastic and prepared a fairly long and well thought-out overview. The fascinating thing about it was that he chose to bring the action to a climax with the sack of Athenree and to omit the last, long journey to Corrib — which is precisely what Maurice Walsh himself had done in the original story "Eudmon Blake", Maurice was interested but had been too scarred by the earlier experience to put any weight behind the project and certainly would not enter into any detailed negotiations. It all came to nought for as Dalton said, the market in swashbuckling films was glutted. Interest revived, however. In 1983 Tom Hayes Films Ltd. took out an option on *Blackcock's Feather*.

The film *Trouble in the Glen* came out in 1954 with Margaret Lockwood and John Laurie. Maurice was asked to assist in the making of it on location in Scotland but refused, being far too sick of the whole business to want any further part in it. He did not like the film either. Incidentally, the original title of the book put forward by Maurice was *Marianna in the Glen* but Chambers persuaded him off that as too "home chat" in flavour. They were right.

That was the end of Maurice's involvement in films. A little later though, in 1957, his friend Neil Gunn concocted a scheme for a joint venture with Maurice to write a screenplay for a film that would cash in on the success of Compton Mackenzie's *Whisky Galore*.

> I have got the whole thing shaped in some 15,000 words — basic English except at crucial points, where actual conversations given. There's a real plot to it, exciting, varied attractive scenes, with the whole whisky process behind it, and through all the kind of romance in which you excel. Now my idea was taking this shape. I would do the whole film script; you would do the novel from it; and we would divide the swag. . . . If all this falls through — which is not unlikely — then I'll type the thing and let you have a look at it for a novel. I think you would enjoy it, for the characters and movements are right into your barrow.[52]

Maurice said he had not a kick left in him for this kind of thing and it shows the extent to which he was disillusioned with the film world, for normally Neil could get him to try his hand at anything. Neil was disappointed.

> We have been in many ploys together and this collaboration on the writing side would be a cornerstone . . . Anyway, think it over, and if you are in the mood for talk, Daisy and I could be coming

over to see you in the first days of October, as before. But now, listen Maurice – if you don't feel like being set upon, just say the word like a good fellow and we'll bide our time until your resources are able to cope with two persons who wouldn't have more than one Irish punch of a night, unless maybe the final small one, of which Daisy has such fond memories. And it's she made me say that. For it's the great concern for you that we have . . . and if you didn't feel like having a shot at the novel – or part of it – to hell with it![53]

Maurice was seventy-eight years old by then, a bit tired and not to be pushed on this. Neil knew it and was concerned for him.

Maurice himself was a bit too early for television, though he gave one interview about his life in Scotland and his interest in the itinerants. At the time of the popular *What's My Line* programme he was approached by Eamonn Andrews to take part in it but refused. Noel Purcell, a friend of Maurice's and a notable Dublin character since the early days when he started as a stooge for Jimmy O'Dea at the Abbey, tried to persuade him but to no avail. Maurice was a private man behind all and had no interest in that kind of public appearance. His public activities had been prolific but essentially serious, whether in connection with the Comhaltas or with the writers' organisation PEN.

The Denis Reeve caricature

Chapter 11. **Politics and PEN.**

Maurice Walsh was an Irish nationalist, not in a blind, unreasoning way but nevertheless with clear sighted conviction. He loved the British people but loathed the British Empire. He was fiercely loyal to his country, whatever professional disagreement he might have with its government, as for example over the salary cut. He was also an author with a growing international reputation and influence. Both his patriotism and his authorship, sometimes together, sometimes separately and not always to his comfort or advantage, took him into the public arena.

His friend Neil Gunn was a Scottish nationalist of long standing as well as a gifted and sensitive author and there was a meeting of minds between the two men on the politics of the Celtic background to both their lives as well as on life and literature in general. After Maurice returned to the Irish Free State, Neil and Daisy Gunn came to visit him fairly often. When de Valera came to power in 1932, Neil brought a party of Scottish nationalists over to visit Ireland and, of course, to see Maurice Walsh. In a memorable evening at St Michael's the group, which consisted of Sir Alexander MacEwan and the Duke of Montrose as well as the Gunns, were entertained royally by the Walsh family. Caroline was a bit overwhelmed by it all but fortunately had her niece Betty Fleming over from Scotland staying with her at the time to help with the preparations. It all went beautifully until Caroline introduced the visitors as Sir Archibald MacLennan and "Mr" Montrose, but nobody minded. It was as good an insight as any into the Irish Free State in action, which is what they had come to see.

Incidentally Compton Mackenzie, who was also involved with the Scottish nationalists and with PEN with Neil Gunn and C. M. Grieve, called on de Valera in 1932 to discuss the idea of a Celtic Commonwealth but got very short shrift from that practical man.

By the early 1930s, Maurice Walsh was well known as a writer and fast becoming Ireland's best selling author. He was an obvious candidate for PEN and became president of the Irish branch in 1938. It was a fairly relaxed organisation and was a thirty-two counties affair, like rugby, so meetings tended to alternate between Dublin and Belfast. PEN stands for:

| Playwrights | Editors | Novelists |
| Poets | Essayists. | |

The position in Ireland in 1938 was:

President: M. Walsh
Vice-Presidents: Patricia O'Connor   D. J. Giltinan
Past Presidents: The Earl of Longford, Rutherford Mayne,
                     Seamus O'Sullivan, Austin Clarke, Kenneth
                     Reddin.

Patricia O'Connor was chairman of the Belfast centre while Maurice was chairman of the Dublin centre.

PEN club activities got Maurice out and about in Ireland and elsewhere. The year he was president, 1938, was particularly busy. He went to America for an international PEN meeting as the Irish delegate and Caroline was able to go with him. They sailed in the *Franconia* and the sea trip did her good. It was a visit to provide lots of echoes later in his books and some vivid memories. They stayed at the Algonquin in New York, where the bartender used to keep a few bottles of beer off the ice for him since Maurice did not like it too cold.

One of the highlights (and disappointments) of the trip was a visit to the White House and tea with the President. Maurice was immensely impressed with Roosevelt but Caroline was shocked by the very thin slices of ham and the slightly stale bread provided for refreshments for the large number of guests. She had expected much better.

Washington in the right season, early in the year, presents a captivating sight at its centre and Maurice loved the spacious elegance of Capitol Hill, with its beautiful and graceful white buildings. (It was his proud boast that he never went to London. The great sprawling size of the place oppressed him, even by hearsay.)

Another highlight of that trip was the chance to meet Eugene Manlove Rhodes and some real cowboys. Will Rogers took to Maurice at once and invited him to a cowboy camp. (The Walshes had some American western connections. Caroline's sister May had married an American called William Dixon and they were living in Bozeman, Montana.) At the camp, Maurice drank "real" coffee made in the cowboy way, strong enough to sole boots with. He recalled the process in one of his books but, of course, added some flavour of his own.

> He emptied the boiling saucepan into the kettle and set the saucepan back over the circle in the range. Maggie skirled.
> "Guidness! Do you want to scaum my good pannie?"
> He held her off with his shoulder and spooned four heaped tablespoons into the hot dry pan, and she wanted to know if he was making a week's supply. The beans had been too long ground and had lost some flavour, so he added two more spoonfuls. He kept it

moving until a spiral of smoke came off, and then poured the boiling water slowly until the fragrant brew frothed to the brim. Then he settled it with a dash of cold water, and drew the pan aside.

"That's all," he said. "Montana camp-fire coffee!"[54]

Maurice loved the whole experience.

Back home he was pressed by Neil Gunn to attend the international PEN meeting in Prague. Neil was thinking of going on to that in June after his own visit to Munich for the publication there of his book *Morning Tide*, but Maurice was too busy.

Towards the end of 1938, however, he was over to Scotland with Richard Hayward for a dinner at the Grosvenor in Glasgow which Scottish PEN gave for its retiring president. Neil Gunn was there too. Maurice had the pleasure of meeting Annie S. Swann. She was sitting between him and one of the English PEN representatives, Gordon Bottomley, at dinner and was charming company, but she had to leave early to drive back to East Lothian so the conversation was relatively short. She sent him one of her books and when he got back to Ireland he sent her a pleasant letter of thanks in his own charming style.

Dear Annie S. Swann,   21.11.38

When I got back from Glasgow, and a day late at that, I was quick off the mark and got in the first word on my red-headed wife. I said: "I sat at dinner with Annie S. Swann and fell in love with her. The grey-brown gleam in her eye would surprise you – a nice dangerous woman." She forgave me with reservations, but the forgiveness was complete when your letter and book arrived. She was born away down in the eighties, and why wouldn't she know Annie Swann? You filled her head so full of dreams and clean romance that a poor Irishman had about as much chance of escape as a snowflake in – you know where. She has recaptured some of that old romance again, and I am almost inclined to forgive you myself.

I did enjoy dinner with you and I am not a bit sorry that you neglected that good man Gordon Bottomley. And what a gallant woman you are to drive your lone for two long hours across the Lowlands low – and you with only a small sherry and something cold inside you. We had our share of what was going ma'am. The speeches were the devil. I had too much soup. An old lowland lady once said to me: "Take plenty of soup; if it is good, it is good for you, and if it isn't you can be sure there is nothing good coming after." . . . We went to the Press Club later in the night and sang rebel

Irish songs and talked dialectic materialism – God help us – and
came home under our own steam, the width of the road no' much
trouble to us. . . . It was fine to meet you, and God bless you, and
may we meet again. The woman-of-the-house sends thanks and
affection. Love I send.

Yours aye,
Maurice Walsh.

They did not meet again, but it was a pleasant little encounter.

In the following year Maurice's friend and fellow author Richard
Hayward became chairman of the Belfast centre of PEN and at the
Belfast dinner that year, 1939, Maurice and David Sears (with whom
Maurice collaborated to write the detective story *The Man in Brown*)
were guests of honour. By then, however, north and south were
beginning to polarise with the approach of war and PEN meetings
looked to be interrupted.

After war did break out life seemed to go on as before for a time.
Maurice was the subject of a gentle caricature by Denis Reeve, a
benign interpretation of a well loved figure. Before long, however, the
literary world was as affected by the war as any other and in the pubs
and restaurants and meeting places as well as in private homes there
was much impassioned discussion of Irish neutrality, but through it
all men like Maurice Walsh were doing all they could to preserve Irish
integrity and dignity and to encourage younger writers to show their
mettle, writers like Seamus Wilmot and Bryan MacMahon. The
Irish Academy of Letters had been founded in 1932 by W. B. Yeats
and George Bernard Shaw, and in January 1940 Sean O'Faolain as
honorary secretary of the academy asked Maurice to be a founder
member of the twenty-one man Council of the Friends of the Irish
Academy of Letters. Their objective was to be "The promotion of
creative literature in Ireland, in Irish or English, by supporting in
every proper way all work of fine intellectual or poetic quality, written
by authors of Irish birth or descent." Maurice was happy to accept
although he missed the inaugural meeting through illness.

Maurice had long been involved with O'Faolain, whose great
magazine *The Bell* became suspect with the authorities after he had
the temerity to criticise the Bishop of Galway. The influence of the
church was very great in all walks of Irish life and people like
O'Faolain and Frank O'Connor were regarded as radicals, a dangerous breed in a very conservative country. Maurice was a little tarred
with the same brush and the fact that he twice left the church told
against him too, even if he did die "in the odour of sanctity" like the
Wolf of Badenoch he used to write about. Maurice's "fault" in official
eyes was that he was always outspoken against hypocrisy wherever he

found it, and that applied to the church as well as any other body. Once in Kerry a neighbour who was very poor was looking forward with eager fervour for her turn to have the stations-mass said in her house – but she did not have the usual £5 donation, to give the priest. No fiver, no stations as it turned out – and Maurice went through the roof when he heard, complaining to the bishop and creating a great fuss. The woman got her stations but it was another black mark for Maurice. In the early book *The Road to Nowhere* he had a dig at priestly money-mongering in his reference to the clergyman who married Jamesy Coffey – "Cannon Mulney, as decent a shepherd as ever cursed a flock, even if he was a bit fond of the dollars" – and that brought him a good bag of protest mail, some of it from his own relatives in Kerry.

Maurice never had an honorary degree from an Irish university, which on the face of it seems an extraordinary omission. Frank O'Connor did not get one either. Institutions then tended to be afraid of living authors and found dead ones safer since they could be guaranteed not to say or do anything embarrassing. Maurice Walsh's own combination of innocence (indeed naivety) in public affairs and mischief was always leading him into situations that the establishment would regard as not quite respectable. For instance, later in the war years he agreed to give a paper to a group that was called "Common Ground", a loose association of artists, writers, thinkers, diplomats and politicians with vaguely ecumenical intentions. It was a serious group with some well known and influential members. Maurice went along and blithely delivered a paper arguing for Mohammed and Islam. He and O'Faolain cooked up the idea between them but it was Maurice who gave the paper and answered all the points and objections – and they were many in a Catholic gathering. No one was quite sure whether he was serious or not.

Maurice worked with O'Faolain even more closely in arguing the case for Irish neutrality. Francis MacManus, the author of *The Greatest of These*, recalled after Maurice's death going into a restaurant to meet O'Faolain during the first year of the 1939-45 war and finding him in heated argument with Maurice. O'Faolain was comparing him as a writer with Robert Louis Stevenson and the modest Maurice was saying that was nonsense. The conversation then turned, as did so many conversations in those ominous days, to Ireland's place in the war and how best to present the case for neutrality to world opinion. They were all worried about a campaign in the American press against the Irish decision to stay aloof and it was O'Faolain who suggested that an article on the subject in the widely read *Saturday Evening Post*, signed by Maurice Walsh, with whose work the *Post* readers were familiar, would be particularly effective. Maurice readily agreed.

The article was dated 1 December 1939 and duly appeared in the *Saturday Evening Post* in January 1940. It was called "Ireland in a Warring Europe". The editor of the *Post* prefaced it with a note which said, somewhat uneasily:

> The creator of Thomasheen James here writes as an Irish patriot. It is for the reader to form his own judgement of the justice and temperateness of his case against Great Britain. In that connection the manuscript was passed by the censorship with minor changes agreed upon between Mr Walsh and the Controller of the Censorship. The altered pages, as the manuscript reached us, bore the initials of both parties.

The original draft of the open letter to the *Post* had run foul of the Irish censor Joseph Connolly because of references to places of possible strategic value along the coastline, especially for submarines, and he wanted those cut out. There were other suggested revisions too and Maurice resisted them. He said that he would rather not publish the article at all than let it go forward in an emasculated form. (He was pleased with "emasculated", a word he got from his son Ian and used gleefully later in his books.) In fact, it well suited the Irish government to let the article go and Connolly wrote to Maurice asking that it should, with the least possible revisions. He agreed.

The article was headed by Maurice's address and began softly.

> There has been much talk of late, in Britain and in America too, of the fallen and tottering small nations of Europe. . . . There has been no word at all of Ireland. And yet Ireland, as far as England and the United States, and possibly Germany, are concerned, is one of the most important small nations in Europe. Small as she is, she is one of the great mother nations and her blood flows in a strong stream – not sluggishly – through the British Empire and many of your states. Possibly this silence has been subtly suggested by the British Foreign Office for its own purposes. The British Foreign Office is quite capable of anything in the game it forever plays, as America ought to know. Well, let us talk of Ireland and be damned to the diplomatic corps. The Lord protect us from harm!

He went on to argue that Ireland had been struggling with considerable success to order its own affairs in its own way over the previous twenty years. The outbreak of war threw its security into doubt and the ideologies of the contestants were so obscure that no matter which side won Ireland might not be permitted to continue as an independent, economic self-reliant unit. He gave a lot of statistics of Irish self-sufficiency (provided by O'Faolain) and said:

I do not say it is all perfect. We love to have our grumble in Ireland and we have high standards. I mention these things merely to indicate that Ireland has been getting on her feet during the past twenty years as a self-supporting country. Of course, some of our huckstering politicians look back on the good old days of huckstering, when our whole economic policy was mere selling and buying, not making; when our well-to-do people in an emptying, emigrant land were cattle jobbers, publican shopkeepers and commercial agents. It is so easy to buy and sell. It takes a man to make, and a huckster never made anything, except excess profits. But it was England's policy to keep us an emigrant country, as she keeps Scotland today – a place where there was the best of food for England, good sport, a simple standard of living for the aborigine – a place to visit in summer and forget in winter. In a word, we were England's floating raft.

He then reminded Americans that they had torn themselves free of the debilitating effect of England in eight years, thanks to the ocean between. Ireland had torn herself partially free in six centuries. And needed to stay free. He dwelt at a little length on Irish culture and said:

We produce, for so small an island, more artists to the square mile than any country in the world – and that is a challenge. In drama, poetry and the novel, we have shown that we are a distinct and a distinguished people. Indeed, I might say that when England lent us her language, we gave her, in return, her literature.

He went on to try to show why it was no more than reasonable that Ireland, having achieved so much, should want to remain neutral now that she had the opportunity for the first time to be neutral. In 1914-18 she had lost 50,000 of her young men, all volunteers, on the promise to John Redmond of a Home Rule Bill which was subsequently denied them. Had it not been for the defiance of Sinn Féin there might well have been conscription in Ireland. The memory of that did not fade and if necessary the people would fight to remain neutral. If occupied they would return to the tactics of 1918-22 when Ireland held at bay fifty-one battalions, six cavalry regiments and a host of police, Black and Tans, official and semi-official agents totalling 60,000 men, through "the old method of the elusive, invisible, resolute ambush and raid". Neither Germany nor England would be able to hold Ireland down without paying a high price for it.

Having given the solemn warning of resistance he then went on to raise the specific grievance of the Irish over the continued occupation of the six northern counties and the deep seated suspicion that they were to be used as the base for the reconquest of the country when the time was ripe. In an atmosphere of invasion, of charge and counter charge, such a suggestion was by no means so preposterous as it seems today. The article went on to point out that the suggestion that the allies went to war in defense of Poland or of some fundamental right made little impression in Ireland when over a million and a quarter Irish people were still held under British rule in the north.

Every man jack of that million and a quarter is Irish, though many of them are bogy-ridden and witch doctor ridden into maintaining a well oiled political machine, run by a clique, in power. You know well what I mean; you known how a corrupt but well organised political machine can rule a city or a country or even a state. By means of this British made machinery, these million and a quarter Irish are in every way as ruthlessly held within the British Empire as were the remaining twenty-six counties, up to the revolt of Sinn Féin and the establishment of the Free State. That puppet parliament · . . has gagged all opposition, interned and imprisoned all who dared to resist, gerrymandered every constituency . . . in every possible way assailed the civil liberties of one third of Ireland's population and then given out to all enquirers that these six counties really like to be ruled that way. Above all, there reigns here the most outrageous religious bigotry imaginable.

If Chamberlain was content for the Sudeten Germans to return to their fatherland, why would he not permit the return of the six counties to their motherland, Ireland? And over it all, what were in fact the war aims of Britain? And what was her attitude to Irish neutrality?

The article ended with a lyrical declaration of faith in the Irish heritage, and a plea for support from America for the preservation of tolerance, charity, restraint and justice.

This little island of ours has seen Europe grow. We may well boast a little. We have helped Europe to emerge from barbarism to civilisation. When the British ran through their woods painted like American Indians, we Irish were making the most delicate, and today priceless, objects of art. We preserved the language and letters of Greece when the Dark Ages had fallen on Europe. The footmarks of Irish scholars all over Europe in those early centuries

– from the fifth to the twelfth – are the signposts of emergent culture on the continent. Through the centuries we have nourished the flame of our own particular philosophy of life. And as we look about us today we ask ouselves whether that flame that we nourish on our modest hearths, in our little island home, may not have some quality of purity and perfection that all the furnaces of the dynasts can never produce. . . . There is here, and many of you have seen it and enjoyed it, a gentle mode of life such as only great age, and innate culture, and high heart, and long experience can create in any land. Austria had it, and she was crushed . . . When all the magnificence that today so allures, enchants and delights in the market places of the great has passed away, what remains most gratefully in the memory of posterity is, I believe, not the sight of even the most lovely and breathtaking relics in a museum, but that which a people leaves as an inheritance to the generations after it, in the way of examples of human courage in defence of all that is gentle and gracious in the human spirit.

It was powerful and emotional stuff and created a great storm. Maurice Walsh found himself inundated with thousands of letters from all over the United States, Canada, Australia and New Zealand and from Britain. The printable suggestions ranged from putting him behind bars to making him president of a United Ireland. There was a lot of support but also a great deal of vituperation. About fifty per cent of those who disagreed about the right of small nations to remain neutral used the epithet "dirty Irish". Variations were of course "bog Irish", "shanty Irish", "black Irish" and "yellow Irish". The volume of poison mail was distressing but not chastening. He replied to those that merited reply, burned the rest and continued to promote the argument.

It was interesting to see how quickly his own and O'Faolain's fears proved correct and a campaign against Irish neutrality grew up in the American press, particularly over the issue of the Irish ports. The Anglo-Irish Treaty of 1921 left England with control of the naval facilities at Queenstown (now Cobh), Lough Swilly in the north in Donegal and Berehaven in Bantry Bay in the south, but an Anglo-Irish agreement in 1938 had handed over ports and facilities unconditionally to the Irish government. The outbreak of war and Ireland's determinedly neutral stance meant that Irish airspace and Irish territorial waters were closed to the warships and aircraft of the belligerent powers. The way that the policy of neutrality was in fact operated has been detailed elsewhere[55] but the ports themselves became a highly emotive issue, particularly when the submarine war against the North Atlantic convoys began to heat up.

Maurice's own position was a strange one in that he believed strongly in Irish neutrality in the war but was passionately proud to have his son Ian a captain in the Royal Army Medical Corps, involved somewhere in the Middle East in the turmoil of war. Neil too went into the RAMC when he qualified and the brothers met in Cairo. But it was by no means a unique position. Many thousands of Irish families had sons and daughters in the British forces or working in factories in Britain and enduring the horrors of the blitz, but there was no doubt that de Valera's determination to keep Ireland out of the war reflected a real national mood. Maurice saw that himself in Dublin but even more clearly when he went back to Kerry, as he did in 1941.

> The mass of the people are really neutral and would fight to maintain neutrality, though we have no illusions as to our chances. But we would keep on fighting. When I was in New York, I met many of the great refugee writers — men like Jules Romain and Thomas Mann — and felt in them, deep under, a terrible depression, a hopelessness, a lack of resiliency. One somehow felt that they would be refugees for a very long time and even get to like it. . . . You can't win the freedom of your country from New York or even from London. We thought we could once on a time, but the little freedom we did achieve was achieved behind our own stone dykes.[56]

Ireland stayed out of the war. Times got harder though. Tea was rationed to two ounces per head per week, coal was very scarce and two gallons of petrol a month was all that the motorists could have, which stopped a lot of movement and did give people a sense of being beleagured.

After the war PEN meetings resumed. Maurice went to the Congress in Edinburgh in 1950 on his way back from a holiday in the Highlands, but found it unstimulating. PEN had started as a friendly, easy going affair, but was becoming over-formalised and he was beginning to be bored with it.

> PEN at Edinburgh was the usual thing, too much dam' talk, especially by the foreigners, who did not know when to stop. By the way, the Scots Covenanters did not cause any trouble. It was the Communists and they were suppressed quickly by their own countrymen. The women were the best of the bunch. Mrs Linklater was just one darling.[57]

Eric Linklater was in the chair at the Edinburgh Congress. Maurice admired his books, as well as his wife, and thought he was "A masterly writer of English, virile and flexible, and a master of character too." Praise indeed.

Back in Dublin literary life was in fact more informal and friendly, with much socialising and informal talk and little in the way of formal literary speeches. Being a relatively small place it was possible to know everyone in the world of art and letters. Art in Dublin had a more human face than in London. In 1942, for example, Maurice met the sculptor Jerome Connor in the Palace bar. A Kerryman from Annascaul, Connor became a sculptor of repute in America and was commissioned to do a monument after the *Lusitania* went down. Many of the bodies had been washed ashore at Cobh and the quay there was thought to be the right place for the monument. Jerome Connor came over, therefore, to do the group known as "The Mourning Fishermen", but when Maurice met him in the Palace he was on his beam ends, short of funds for his work and in some personal distress. Two of his figures in bronze, cast but unfinished, were at the Hammond Lane Foundry. These were big figures, over six feet high. Maurice took charge of his fellow Kerryman and after getting him straightened out joined with David Frame of the Hammond Lane Foundry in Pearse Street, Dublin, in financing the completion of the monument that stands at Cobh today.

Dublin was and is a friendly place. Maurice entertained a lot and was himself entertained. As the years went by he kept his inner circle of close friends from the Excise days but made some new ones and had a huge range of acquaintances all over the country. People like the poet Paddy Kavanagh were often at the house. He used to see Brendan Behan quite often, usually in the Palace bar. Behan would enfold Maurice in his great arms and hail him as "the doyen of Irish riters" in a huge loud voice. Maurice admired Behan's great vitality: "a decent stick of a fellow, a rough diamond who is not as rough as he looks or acts."[58]

Not all was friendliness, charity and good fellowship, however. There was a nasty incident in 1953 when Maurice was in Belfast for a PEN dinner, having brought as his guest a 1916 man.[59] Neil Gunn was there too. The PEN club, as an all-Ireland organisation, had always carefully avoided religion and politics in speeches and avoided embarrassment by not having any national anthem, Irish or British, played at their dinners. At the 1953 International PEN Congress dinner, however, north/south politics were introduced, the loyal toast called for and "God Save the Queen" played. Maurice and his guest sat impassively through toast and anthem but the incident caused grave embarrassment and Maurice was furious. He was using a stick at the time to help him get about and he stomped out of the room thumping it on the floor in rage and shouting, "Wan battalion, that's all we need to clear up this place!"

Shortly after that he received a parcel from Belfast addressed to

"Malice Walsh" and found in it a slashed and mutilated copy of *And No Quarter*. It saddened him immensely to be the object of such a sick attack. "Ah, we're a different breed," he said.

The old, easy friendship of writers seemed to have gone for good. Young writers were producing works that read like translations from the Russian and storytelling as an art, for the time at any rate, was dead.

Part 4.

Savouring.

An Assessment.

Chapter 12. **The Storyteller**

Maurice Walsh described his books as "yarns" in his own modest way and used to speak of writing books rather than novels. The distinction is an interesting one and modest though Maurice undoubtedly was, in public and in private, the spinner of yarns could justifiably show pride rather than modesty in presenting his tales, for the role of the traditional storyteller was in some ways more complex and yet less pretentious than is that of the modern novelist.

The storyteller was part poet, part historian, part entertainer, a craftsman with words and occasionally also with music, which he used to elaborate and embroider his basic story. He worked deftly through a combination of character and incident, giving full rein to each as it appeared during the unfolding of his tale but taking great pains to weave the right atmosphere round people and action as he went along. It was the essence of the art that the listener did listen, gripped and carried along from start to finish. That is not to say that the story had to be all pace and action. The variety of tempo and mood might have been well nigh infinite, but the inwardness of the novel, particularly of what we have come to call the psychological novel, was absent.

In this chapter, I propose to look at Maurice Walsh's achievement as a storyteller. I shall not be looking for any psychological analysis either of the characters or the author himself. Maurice indeed was fond of saying, when he wanted to be provocative, that there was "no such thing as psychology as a science. The mind is not an entity. The mind, or the soul if you like, is only a process, same as digestion."[60]

In relation to his books, storytelling by Maurice Walsh was very much a natural process in that the author speaks simply and directly to the reader and draws him into plot and description as easily as breathing. The stories themselves do not lack psychological insights, but those come to the surface only in retrospect. The characters certainly develop in relation to each other, through what they do and where they do it. In all Maurice's books *place* is very important. His characters are drawn firmly and vividly, his dialogue sparkles, his actions bowl along at a cracking pace, but behind all it is the descriptions and the evocations of places that give his books their extraordinary richness. Whatever place he uses, the heroes take strength from it and the villains are weakened by their lack of ties to it or understanding of it. That is a powerful earth magic.

I want to contrast your young land with this old one that has been peopled for ten thousand years – or thirty thousand. It has been closely peopled too, and has absorbed the mentality of many races. Man is no longer himself here. He belongs to the place. There is some subtle evocation – aura is better – some subtle aura of old times and old ways, old wisdoms – old wickednesses also – that affect and claim a man: that are wholly satisfying and make life intensive in spite of all external sameness.[61]

It is fundamental to Maurice's stories, perhaps to the Scottish ones in particular, that the place – its history and experience and the lingering influence of all that has gone before – goes to make the people who live in it and speaks to the people who visit it or pass through it, if they can hear. Think of Glencoe.

The two places dearest to the heart of this storyteller were his adopted Highlands and his native Kerry.

> Glounagrianaan! that widest, sunniest trough of all the valleys raying out from the Four Churches, green with short grass, grey with limestone, alive with the sound of birds singing and water cascading down the wide aprons! Serene hollow below high hills of heather where sheep were dotted like pale brown stones – with low white houses strung along a winding grey road, the little town at the mouth of the glen, and Hugh's school nearby, and, beyond, the sea lifting to the horizon![62]

Scotland and Kerry. Both sang to Maurice, vivid in his mind's eye, intense in his recollection, flowing vividly through his pen on to the pages of his books. They appear in his stories virtually as characters in their own right and he set in those places that he loved people he had known in reality, in reading or in imagination: the gallant men and the blackguards, the fighting men and the priests, fishermen and farmers, tinkers and noblemen, foreigners and natives, idealised often but always human. And somehow vision and reality become congruent in his books, as they must have done for rapt audiences listening to the storytellers of long ago.

It is interesting to compare the significance of place in Maurice Walsh's books and those of his friend Neil Gunn. Neil became steadily more mystical, indeed transcendental, in the thoughts expressed in his carefully structured and delicately written novels in a way that the storyteller Maurice never did; but the sense of the living countryside, the place with all its history and aspirations welling up in it is almost painfully intense in such books as *Morning Tide* and *Highland River*. Gunn's Highland scene has a starkness that makes the Walsh vision seem lush in comparison, perhaps the difference between Caithness and Moray though Neil Gunn was generally a far more austere writer; but the significance of the place in both writers' books, as more than just a convenient setting for the action, was very similar. Neil Gunn managed to convey the intense feeling of mountain and glen, to let the reader hear the very heartbeat of the land, by introducing it through the eyes and the ears and the mind of a young boy. The device works perfectly. Maurice never wrote of children or youths, except perhaps fleetingly in the case of Daheen Coffey in *The Road to Nowhere* or Dinny Lane in *Castle Gillian*, where the boys are more important in relation to the adult characters than as characters in their own right. There is also little Alsuin in *Trouble in the Glen* but that child is old beyond her tender years. No, Maurice did not make use of the fresh vision of the child, perhaps because his own vision was so rich.

Maurice Walsh's literary output comprised twenty books, some poetry, a play and a variety of articles, for example on whisky or on the province of Moray. It is the books I am concerned with here.

They divide into five groups, although the subdivisions are a bit artificial and overlap to some extent. However, they are:

Those set in Scotland;
Those set in Ireland;
Historical or folklore settings;
Short story collections;
Detective stories.

The Scottish group provided the richest harvest in numbers at least, with six full length books. These were *The Key Above the Door* (1926), *While Rivers Run* (1928), *The Small Dark Man* (1929), *The Hill is Mine* (1940), *The Spanish Lady* (1943) and *Trouble in the Glen* (1950).

The Key Above the Door, as we know from Maurice's letters (see Chapter 7), was a deliberate attempt to recreate the atmosphere and "glamour" of the Highlands he loved, written in Dublin while he was separated from his family who were still in Scotland. He peopled his story with characters based very much on individuals he knew and he put those characters into a lifestyle that was in part his own and in part what he would have liked it to be. Having decided on the tone he lives it in the pages of the book and makes the reader want to share it and to see and touch and smell and taste the very atmosphere of the setting.

The story itself is a simple one. Tom King and his two friends get into trouble in a poaching ploy on the Leonach River with the high handed, autocratic villain of the piece Edward Leng, who has taken the local estate for the season. King and Leng are attracted to the same woman and eventually fight over her in the climax to the story. The small Celtic hero, sib to the land and the people, thrashes the southerner Leng, a big man but with a weak, eastern strain in him. The story is as simple as that but the book is filled with incident and the whole is set against the panoramic sweep of the "wide province of Moray" and the stark majesty of Skye, where the vistas of mountain and sea are described with breathtaking eloquence.

> The sun was in the west, and the sea was a shimmering plain of gold, with the whale-back islands of Canna and Rum standing dead-black out of the shimmer. Below the high black cliffs of Macleod's Tables stood the pinnacles of the Seven Sisters with uneasy water about their deep planted feet, and at the horizon stretched the long, purple shadow of the Outer Isles – Uist, Barra and Benbecula. Behind me spread the rolling, ruddy moors, pierced here and there by bold limestone bluffs, towered over by the Cuchullins, and suffused with light – austere moors, brooding, mystic, changeless, uncaring. [63]

The characterisation is deftly handled, particulary the interplay between King and his close friend Neil Quinn and the slow, subtle dignity of Archie MacGillivray. The fine, clean, enduring friendship of men is triumphantly described in this book but the developing love between King and Agnes de Burc is delicately portrayed, slow and inevitable though at first unrecognised by the two and then resisted by both of them, but with complete certainty in the reader (or the listener) about how it all must end. The critical scene when Tom King and Archie MacGillivray set themselves to keep Agnes de Burc alive through the cold of the night after they are marooned on the Wolf of Badenoch's island in Loch Ruighi is movingly done. The three of them, and Leng, have all been soaked after their boat over-turned and have done what they can to dry themselves, but the woman is shivering and Leng is pacing up and down determinedly to keep himself alive. King sits with his back to the ruined wall, out of the autumn wind, with Agnes on his knees, her back against Archie's.

> Her hands were very cold. I covered them with one of mine, threw open my old brown jacket so that my chest was bare, and pulled her round so that she almost faced me. As I drew her hands forward she resisted for a moment, and then yielded with a little sudden intake of breath. For I placed her cold hands on my body under my arms – and I did not feel the cold. Her hands moved a little, and were still; and, her head being against my shoulder, I heard her long sigh.
>
> "This is – too exquisite," she whispered. "What life-force you have, you strong man – and your skin is like velvet."
>
> I had no reply to that, but she must have felt the strong beating of

the heart that was warming her and me.[64]

Overall this is a story told in a straightforward but charming style, interspersing philosophy (without pedantry) and high humour and clean romance with fishing and shooting and the development of the action towards the inevitable savage fight at the climax. The whole is set against the pure Highland scene whose freshness and vitality illuminates every chapter. The author has a painter's eye for a scene but each graphic description of mountain or loch comes from the heart. It is easy to understand why Barrie was so taken with it.

The second book Maurice published was also in the Scottish group. *While Rivers Run* has broadly the same Highland setting and uses some of the same characters in minor roles – Tom and Agnes King and Archie MacGillivray. But it introduces a wider range of characters, including an American heir to a Scottish estate and a sardonic, humourous Irishman, Paddy Joe Long, who naturally comes from Kerry. He was to appear again in the one of the Irish books, *The Road to Nowhere*.

In *While Rivers Run* the conflict between the characters is not so elemental and the love interest is split. Alistair MacIan and Don Webster vie for the attention of the actress Norrey Carr. MacIan falls instead for the Scottish girl Margaret Brands but fights with Webster in the end anyway. The inimitable Paddy Joe marries Norrey, as we all knew he would (though we were a bit worried that he might let her go). There is little plot, as such, just a group of people working out their relationships with each other and with the place they happen to be in. The theory of place is made quite explicit in this book, both in the growing recognition by the young American heir MacIan of the importance and worth and fascination of his uncle's forestry project and, more significantly, through the mouth of Willie Raasay who lives in the wilderness called Larach na Gael.

I am by way of thinking sometimes it was a kind of sanctuary, the same as you'll get in the deer forests – only a sanctuary for men. A place where the clans kept a truce, and a good many of them joined lands about here – and always tulzieing at that. But it is no' the exact thing to say the place is haunted – 'tis only the feel of the place, ye ken.[65]

By contrast there is an interesting passage describing a journey across London which some of the protagonists make – purely an interlude but put in to point the contrast with the Highlands.

The people around them, the people that bobbed past the windows, were all of a character, set in the same mould, steeled in the same indifference, devastating, heart-breaking, impervious, awe-some – gregarious without being intimate, withdrawn yet huddled in herds, alive yet apparently without soul – and all grasping evening papers.[66]

And this from a man who had never been in London in his life, let alone travelled in the rush hour!

Incidentally there are some good individual stories within the larger one, little tales told by Paddy Joe Long that stand alone, though they have never been collected in a separate volume. They include the story of the Kerry Blue terrier and the stern but uplifting tale of the lonely Maire MacCarthy. Maurice himself, towards the end of his life, thought about bringing these little tales together and perhaps adding to them, but the idea came to nothing.

With the third book in the Scottish group (and the third published) we see the power of the storyteller reaching to full maturity. *The Small Dark Man* is a vivid tale, swiftly but subtly told, enlivened by rich imagination and experience. The technique is masterly and although the plot is once again very simple, the characterisation has great and telling depth and the atmosphere building is intense. Hugh Forbes, the small dark man of the title, is a schoolmaster in Kerry but is on holiday in Scotland to visit his friend from the Great War, Tearlath Grant. Tearlath has a sister called Frances Mary and a friend called Allison Ayre. After some misunderstanding Tearlath and Allison and Hugh and Frances Mary end up together. In between there is an overbearing (but big and strong) cousin called Vivian Stark to be taught a lesson or two. Yet that simple structure underlies a richly satisfying tale with strong characters and great pace.

Hugh Forbes is a masterpiece, a small, resolute, quirky, steadfast, humorous individual with a deep and sensitive nature and vast pride of race. His coming to Innismore sets the place awhirl from his earliest meeting with Frances Mary and the arrogant Stark. This is a dominant hero, fierce in his strength but with imaginative insight and surprising tolerance. In the beginning of the story he realises that Frances Mary is his friend's sister, though he believes that he is not known to her or Stark and does not tell her. Stark forces him out of the hut where Frances Mary is resting with a blistered heel but, out of earshot, Hugh Forbes wrestles the big man into a few falls and sends him on his way by a combination of force and reason but does not tell Frances Mary that either. (A close one, Hugh, for all his easy tongue.) Later Frances Mary traps him into admitting the struggle, and when he passes it off as nothing, asks why Stark had a broken collar bone.

Suddenly, he felt a little surge of heat go through him, and that steadied him. This man, when really angry, was anything but ebullient. He did no more than lean forward towards her and look at her, but the shock of those level eyes made her shrink within herself.

"I did not set out to break his collar-bone, woman dear." His voice drawled deeply. "I am sorry I broke his collar-bone. It was his neck I was trying to break."

He lifted his open hand before her eyes, and she drew back an inch, her eyes failing to focus on the spread of fingers.

"And look here, my fine partisan; you can tell that long man of yours that the next time he lays a finger on me I'll drive that hand through his breast-bone, and feed his pea-nut of a heart to a hound-pup."

"Oh!" said Frances Mary.[67]

But, of course, Frances Mary is not silenced for long. (The girl, incidentally, was based very much on Maurice's niece Betty Fleming, and in Betty's own copy of the book Maurice wrote the remark Hugh Forbes made on first seeing Frances Mary: "She has good legs on her, that one." Frances Mary's mother, the near blind and near psychic Caroline Grant, owed much to Toshon's mother Grannie Begg. That character too is finely drawn and the sense of immediate rapport between her and Hugh is very sensitively brought out.)

The book teems with incident and atmosphere, such as the description of the local games at Glenmart and the contest between Hugh and his friend Tearlath at the big stone. The tension is built up piece by piece inexorably, just as the two men draw out their reserves putt by putt to add inches to their previous throw. And the final fight with Stark is a mouth drying affair. The whole book is one to read from start to finish at a sitting and then start again to savour slowly.

After *The Small Dark Man*, the fourth Maurice Walsh book was an even more exciting one, *Blackcock's Feather*; but it was to be eleven years before another Scottish book appeared and that was *The Hill Is Mine* in 1940. Maurice Walsh had been to a number of international PEN meetings and had been to America in 1938, so he had been absorbing impressions of people from other countries. He had introduced an American to Scotland in *While Rivers Run* but Alistair MacIan was a very anglicised young man. In *The Hill is Mine* the American is more fully drawn. It is a light tale in which Stephen Wayne from Bozeman, Montana (the home of Maurice's niece Jeannie Begg Dixon) comes to Scotland to see the croft of Balmerion which came to him on the death of his grandmother. The hard-headed but gallant Westerner soon succumbs to the magic of the country and its people and he finds a wife. But Maurice's stories were no longer quite that simple. While the hero seems set fair to marry young Marion Finlay, the daughter of the old and impoverished laird, it is the more interesting older woman, the vivid but also poor English aristocrat Lady Alice Tromes, that he ends up with.

This is a pleasant, gentle story set against the background of the old order being dispossessed but the old ways and loyalties clinging on tenaciously. It is written with delicacy and sympathy, especially in those passages dealing with the recurrent madness of the old laird and the strain on his daughter. There is no villain and not a lot of action and while this mellow tale is neatly executed and pleasantly told it is by no means one of Maurice Walsh's more memorable books.

The Spanish Lady appeared in 1943. It was the fifth book in the Scottish group and can be described as memorable by any standards. Maurice himself referred to it as "the last squeeze of the bag and I have no more sentimental juices left, thank the Lord. I found the writing of it too hard. Day after day you cannot pull things out of empty air and trust entirely to your memory." [68] Nevertheless his memory of the Highland scene was in no way dimmed or blunted by the absence enforced by the war. The descriptions are as crisp and fresh as ever. It is also one of his best books for inventive characterisation.

Diego Usted from Paraguay, a captain in a commando unit, comes sick from the war to the remote glen where his Scottish mother was born to see a maternal uncle he has never met and to die quietly among his own, if that is to be the way for him. There he meets Ann Mendoza from out of the Basque country with her own sorrow behind her and married to a man twice her age, Major-General Harper, head of the Home Guard and laird in Glen Affran, who is actively trying to break the entail. When he is murdered Diego and Ann fall separately under suspicion since they are found on the scene of the crime with Diego trying to make the death look like suicide. Through the resourcefulness of the men of the glen, however (and the second sight of Diego's aunt Big Ellen), the truth is brought out and the glen settles the matter in its own way. The book could fairly be called Maurice Walsh's first crime story but it is not a thriller in the usual sense and has no detective. Besides, the essential Scottish flavour puts it firmly into the Scottish group.

Ann Mendoza Harper is one of Maurice Walsh's most interesting heroines. In the early books the older women, the matriarchs, are more strongly drawn than the heroines but with Ailish Conroy Trant in *The Road to Nowhere*, Meg Anderson in *And No Quarter* and perhaps also the shy Dairne in *Sons of the Swordmaker*, his young women become much more complex and more interesting characters. Alice Tromes in *The Hill is Mine* is a minor character but has more individuality than Marion, the laird's daughter. With Ann Mendoza, however, Maurice Walsh had created a mature, vibrant woman with a strength of personality to match that of the book's hero and touch of foreign mystery about her besides.

One of the striking achievements in this book is the way Maurice captures the cadence of Spanish speech. It is, for example, very telling when Diego, treated with insolent hostility and suspicion on his first encounter with the arrogant General Harper, stands on his own dignity and says: "Go thou to hell!" The speech of Ann Mendoza is even more Spanish in texture: "It is my regret that you should be questioned with rudeness in this glen where your people live who are my friends."[69]

Maurice himself always wanted to see Spain, but although some of the knowing references in his books suggest that he did so in fact he never got there. He may have picked up some of the flavour of Spain and the rhythms of Spanish speech from his reading of Hemingway but he also got a lot from a friend called Jim Talbot. Talbot, who was a student at Trinity at the same time as Maurice's son Ian (although he was twenty years older), had spent some years in South America where, amongst other things, he had been a gaucho. He used to tell Maurice about the pampas and the haciendas and on one occasion persuaded him to try the fierce drink maté, drunk in the traditional way out of a gourd. Maurice thought it tasted like hot varnish but in the book he tells of the custom of passing round the maté gourd in the afternoons with the assurance of one brought up to it.[70]

There is a nice personal note in the book when Big Ellen, Diego's aunt, is telling him about her own scattered family and says of one of her sons, " . . . and Ian, who is little, is a doctor in the Canal Zone."[71] Maurice's son Ian, who was little, was in fact at that time a doctor in the RAMC in the Canal Zone.

Trouble in the Glen, the last book in the Scottish group, also has a Spanish flavour although it is altogether a lighter book than *The Spanish Lady*. Sir Gawain Micklethwaite, flyer, returns after the war to Glen Easan to find trouble between the new laird, a South American grandee with Scottish ancestry, and the men of the glen. Alsuin, the young but ailing daughter of his friend David Keegan, puts a "task" on him to set things right and he does, with alarms and excursions but ultimate success. There is no really nasty villain in this story, though there is still a good fight at the end. The heroine Iosabel Mengues has fire but lacks the depth and subtlety of Ann Mendoza. The most interesting characters are the tinkers, old Parlan MacFee and his dwindling tail, and Sanin Cejador y Mengues himself, an unbending hildago but one with wisdom and vision.

The Scottish group of books contain much of the humour and warmth of the author himself and are, for the most part, superbly told stories with vivid atmosphere and rich imagery. They are stories of the outdoors, of hill and river and glen, and the choice of language and structure reflects that.

They also contain much of the Walsh poetry. Maurice loved poetry but would not presume to call himself a poet and, in a sense, played down his verses by inserting them at different places in his books rather than attempting to let them stand alone. They are certainly good enough to stand apart in a collection but are also fitting in their context in the books, from humour to high seriousness.

In *The Key Above the Door* when Tom King has to abandon an icy conversation with the villain Leng because his bees decide to swarm, he leaps about his garden, squirting water on the swarming bees to make them settle, singing all sorts of snatches, such as the old nursery rhyme:

> There was an old woman tossed up in a blanket seventy times as
>   high as the moon.
> Where she was going I couldn't but ax her, for in her hand she
>   carried a broom.
> "Old 'oman, old 'oman, old 'oman," says I,
> "Where are you going up so high?"
> "To sweep the cobwebs offn the sky,
> An I will be with ye tomorrow, by-'m-by." [72]

That has an infectious gaiety about it, a jerky rhythm too, to match the leaps around the garden amidst the swarming bees.

Later Tom King the confirmed batchelor sings his own philosophy, with the seeds of doubt already stirring. This is no traditional song, but Walsh the poet.

> If I did own the silver moon as well as golden sun,
> With Jupiter and Saturn, and planets one by one,
> And Sirius, that great dog-star, and mighty belt Orion,
> I'd long for still some wee small sun that never yet did shine.
>
>
> Had I fashioned all the roses that ever bloomed in June,
> The marigold, the daffodil, the heather, and the broom,
> The shy, retiring violet, and canna bawn ablown,
> I'd long for still some wee small bud whose seed was never sown.
>
>
> Had I the choice of all the queenly ones that ever troubled man —
> Helen, Cleopatra, and Mary's mother Anne —

I'd sell my choice for ae bawbee and gang the road my lone,
For the Quoine was never born I would care to call my own. [73]

That has a lyrical resonance that runs pleasantly. Maurice's son Neil
set the piece to music.

The Small Dark Man has a lot of verse, introducing each chapter and
popping up at appropriate moments. Hugh Forbes himself is inclined
to burst into song.

No home have I, no dear one,
No friend, no kin to cheer one,
No foe to fight or fear one,
Nowhere to go or stay;

My life is reft of laughter,
My clan gone down in slaughter,
Yet in some dim hereafter
Is dawning of the day. [74]

That is Hugh Forbes without a care, awander, with his inner thoughts
coming to the surface of a seemingly placid life. Later, though, he
sings the song of a man with a sore heart, and him brave.

The dawn and the dusk are the same,
And wine it inspires me no longer.
To play at and fail at the game
And be blithe I would need to be stronger
Than Finn or Cuchulain or Conal.

But maybe next year or next life
The wine will have flavour and savour,
And beauty shall pierce like a knife,
And in war I would laugh at a favour
From Finn or Cuchulain or Conal.

And again a love I may find
Like the dusk of the dawn and the gloaming,
To take me and break me and grind,
And set me again to the roaming
With Finn and Cuchulain and Conal. [75]

As Maurice Walsh himself says in the book: "That air came out of
the deeps of life and every note vibrated in the heart's strings."

This is the true poet, the maker, weaving his spells. The words, the sense, the names, the invocation and the very rhythm have marvellous and sonorous power.

While Rivers Run produced a crop of songs and snippets of verse, usually from the irrepressible Paddy Joe Long and often out of Maurice's own childhood memories. Some are moving, some are sad and some very amusing.

> For Ale it has a pleasing bite,
> And Wine a soothing smooth,
> And Usquebaugh a blinding light
> That gleams on naked truth.
> But ale and wine and usquebaugh
> Have lost their taste to me
> Since she to whom I'm tied by law
> Drinks my share of the three. [76]

The Spanish Lady has some humorous verse, too, and a good drinking song, but the best item comes from the lips of Ann Mendoza Harper, the proud woman of the Basques, with a song of great vigour and rhythmic intensity.

> Grey falcon, in my wrist do you dare set a claw?
> > Claw then! Claw then!
> Don Cupid, to my heart your arrow would you draw?
> > Draw then! Draw then!
> For my hand is cased in leather 'gainst claw and wind and weather,
> But my heart is soft, unguarded, unwise, unaware, unwarded.
> > So I laugh then, and I fall then.
> Old grey Time, on my head do you sift your snow?
> > Snow then! Snow then!
> Kingly Death, where you lead, must I go where you go?
> > Go then! Go then!
> For my head is fast declining, my eyes soon lose their shining,
> While my heart, still softly warm, knows my face has lost its charm.
> > So I weep then, and I sleep then. [77]

There is power and poignancy there, of the highest order of literary expression. By 1943 Maurice Walsh was surer of himself, prepared to let his poetic muse run with more freedom and as a result wrote verse with fluency and assurance, power and persuasiveness. The pity is that he did not write more of it.

The last book in the Scottish group, *Trouble in the Glen*, has very little verse but a good tinkers' song.

Our road, it is a long, lone road
That nowhere has an end.
It turns away from house and fold
Where no man is our friend.
And all we own is that long road
Where once we owned the Glen,
And we'll seek it, and we'll keep it – and to hell with settled
    men![78]

The Irish group contains four books, although again this classification is somewhat arbitrary and overlaps with other groups – the short story collections, for example. However, the four are *The Road to Nowhere* (1934), *Green Rushes* (1935), *Castle Gillian* (1948) and *A Strange Woman's Daughter* (1954).

Maurice Walsh introduced an Irishman into his first book *The Key Above the Door*, although Neil Quinn was in fact based on his friend from Caithness, Neil Gunn, so perhaps that should not count. *While Rivers Run* produced a more developed Irishman, from Kerry at that, in Paddy Joe Long. Much of what that highly individualistic gentleman has to say is autobiographical Walsh reminiscence. The third book though introduced the most vigorous Irish character to date, Hugh Forbes. Up to that point the Irishmen had all been introduced in a Scottish setting (and were none the worse for that) but in his fourth book, *Blackcock's Feather*, Maurice reversed the process and brought a Scot to Ireland. That book is considered later, in the historical group, but it certainly qualifies as Irish too. However, in the first book in the Irish group I have defined, the fifth published, the same technique is used in a somewhat different way. Rogan Stuart, who in his time played stand-off half for Scotland, loses himself in Ireland in a tinker's garb as Rogue McCoy, tinker's curate to Jamesy Coffey, king of the roads, and in doing that finds himself again.

Paddy Joe Long and Alistair MacIan, now married and settled down with their wives after *While Rivers Run*, appear again briefly and start the wheels of fate rolling when they adopt the passing Rogan Stuart into their camp. Stuart is a quiet man, touched with sorrow, but with a strong fibre. His great fight with the black captain Eudmon Butler comes in the middle of the book instead of at the end and this time it is described at one remove, as it were, by Jamesy Coffey giving evidence in court afterwards. The tale loses nothing in the telling. Jamesy is the star of the book, a colourful king of the roads with his own unshakeable standards and code of conduct. The tinker scenes are vividly painted, from the little camp where Rogue grows in stature and responsibility to the roadmen's pub where the best company is found and the finest stories can be heard. And of course the scene is

Kerry, high wide and handsome, described, or perhaps painted is the better word, with love. The very action starts on the shoulder of Slievemaol, looking down the length of Dounbeg Bay as far as the narrows of Corullish with Hugh Forbes' own Glounagrianaan inland. There are descriptions of Listowel and references to Ballydonoghue and to John Walsh himself.

This book is a gem. It has the full blooded mix of hero and villain, a heroine of strength, a fast moving plot and lots of high romance and adventure, all told in a lyrical and flowing narrative. It is not surprising that so many different people saw the possibility of a film version and went to the length of writing screenplays. It is a pity that no film was ever made. As Maurice himself said, Barry Fitzgerald would have been a natural for the part of Jamesy Coffey.

The following year, 1935, introduced *Green Rushes*, the collection of five short stories linked through Hugh Forbes, the small dark man, in the days when he led a flying column in the Black and Tan war. The title has its origin in an old Gaelic love saying – "I will lay green rushes under her feet that she may step softly" – and that is what Hugh Forbes promises Margaid MacDonald when she and her brother Major Archie MacDonald are by accident made prisoners of the flying column in the first story, "Then Came the Captain's Daughter". Each story relates the romance of a different person, though not Hugh's own. His red-headed woman was waiting for him in the future, at Innismore in Scotland. The stories are set mainly in Kerry during and after the Black and Tan troubles and are again of the open air. Most of them appeared in magazines before they were brought out in book form and the book itself suffers from not being part of an original whole. "The Quiet Man" is the best of the five, a deftly structured, beautifully told story of the quiet, strong, sensitive man forced at last to show his strength against the brute. The build up to the final fight with Red Will Danaher has the quality of epic, slow and inexorable with the wings of fate hovering over all the whole time. This is a tale which combines the best elements of the storyteller's art, the essential simplicity of style with a richly musical language.

"Then Came the Captain's Daughter" is well told, though it is not in the same class as "The Quiet Man" except for the story within the story, the haunting tale told by Mickeen Oge Flynn of little Ellen Molouney, whose father came back from the grave to protect and comfort his own. It is a fairy story of poignant beauty and great tenderness.

Ellen Oge Molouney, all her days – and they were many – kept close about her the memory of that walk through the July night. It was as happy as walking in a king's garden with a king's son, and love in the songs of birds; as long and as short as a fine story and it well told; as pleasant as May morning and the blackbird lilting his one tune; it was as quiet as that June hour before the sun sets into the solitudes of the gloaming stealing gently; it was as unhurried as a noneen opening in the dew; timeless as a dream.

She could never tell the roads they came or the places that she saw. Indeed, they came no made roads at all. Their feet moved over dewy grass where the gossamer was like pearly threads on the green; along hedgerows where small birds saluted them with drowsy cheeps; under tall, straight trees, standing to attention column by column, where the rays of moonlight striking through were finer than white silver; along small streams that came out under dark bushes to gurgle and gleam at them over clean gravel. That is all she remembered of that journey in the night. In the distance dogs barked or howled forlornly at the moon, and the white houses glimmered along the hillside. But they themselves moved in a world apart, in a dimension of their own, using time and space to suit the content that filled them. And no cock crew.

They were in no hurry. Often they rested by stream and hedgerow, and the tall man talked to the little maid, softly, gently, with a tenderness beyond all tears. He told her tales she knew and tales she did not know; and he got her to display her artless young heart, and that he cherished with a pride finer than the pride of all victories, all glories, all defeats. But alas! The night went on, nevertheless, and happiness will not abide forever under the sky. The moon was setting and a vivid whiteness streaming up in the north-east when, at last, they came out in the open road above the Feale Bridge. And there the tall man stopped Ellen Oge, his hand lightly on her shoulder.

"There, then, is the Feale River, girleen, and that is Listowel town beyond on the slope. You know where you are now?"

"Oh yes, sir! That's Cnucanor Hill in front of us."

"Here then we part." His voice was deep and low. "The dawn is here, and we cannot keep cocks from crowing, for the cocks have to crow in every dawn. You will have to hurry now, Ellen Oge." He ran his hand gently down the nape of her neck and gave her a little push between the shoulders. "Run, a leanaveen! your mother will be waiting for you."

Lightly, then, she ran down on to the bridge. And away out on the island farm a cock crew, and his clarion was as keen and as sad as the horns of fairyland. At the middle arch she turned to wave farewell. The road was empty.[79]

Love is stronger than death, Maurice would say, and that beautiful tale of a father's love for his child is a perfect gem of the storyteller's art.

The rest of the stories in the book are of lesser quality and "The Red Girl" is a bit out of place. It is as near to a clumsy tale as Maurice ever told. What these stories tend to suffer from is the defect Neil Gunn put his finger on astutely, the clash between the storyteller's knowledge of what is right for his muse and the professional author's knowledge of the sort of material his magazine editors want. They were by no means always the same. Maurice Walsh himself was also a sentimental man and in some of his stories the sentiment took over and twisted coincidence to ensure the happy ending. Moreover, the depth of his imagery remained as rich as ever and sometimes the plots were just too weak to support the weight.

The third book in the Irish group came out in 1948. *Castle Gillian* was originally to be called *The Damsel Debonair* or *Waiting is Good Hunting* or even *A Man for Castle Gillian*. Most of the story had been conceived when Maurice was trying to turn *The Road to Nowhere* into a screenplay. The ingredients are familiar, the small man and the bully, two different love interests, some beguiling tinkers – and a Scotsman, Robin Morrison, who comes into the Irish racing stables and starts events moving towards their climax. The book is not an outstanding one but the writing seems effortless and the characterisation is sharp and wholly convincing. The minor characters, particularly the tinkers, are well drawn, significant to the plot and arresting in the conversations without being intrusive. They "fit". The fight between Gillian Morris and Garrett Ward, the villain, is very exciting and highly individualistic. Most of Maurice's fights followed the same broad pattern yet every one is distinctive.

The last book in the Irish group, *A Strange Woman's Daughter*, was published in 1954. It is a curious work, rather rigid in structure for Maurice Walsh and showing its origins as a play. Young Mary Keane lives with Hannah Dillane and loves her son Michael who is apparently mad since having a vision at the lakeside. Hannah's sister Margaret Gannon is reputed to be mad, having been wandering the roads all her adult life. The whole thing resolves itself in the end in a predictable but not very convincing ending. There are some telling scenes in Gorah madhouse, with three exceptionally lucid patients who emerge as far more aware and wise than the pedantic asylum superintendent. Notwithstanding that, the book cannot be regarded as a success.

The third group of books, the historical romances and folklore stories, contains Maurice Walsh's greatest achievements as a writer, a poet and a storyteller. The four books are *Blackcock's Feather* (1932), *And No Quarter* (1937), *Sons of the Swordmaker* (1938) and *Son of Apple* (1947).

Blackcock's Feather is still used as a text book in Irish schools for the high quality of its English prose and it has been hailed as one of the finest historical romances ever written. Even in its earliest form, as the story "Eudmon Blake, or The Sack of Athenree", serialised in the *Irish Emerald* in 1908, it was recognised as an exceptional example of the great storyteller's art.

Briefly, David Gordon, out of Auchindoun in Scotland, comes after the death of his father to visit his cousin (on his mother's side) Donal Ballagh O'Cahan at Dungiven in Ulster. David has spent his youth and many weary years with his dour father, one of Mary Stuart's Highland hawks, who taught swordplay on the fringes of the armies of Europe to eke out a living while waiting for the tide to turn against Elizabeth and allow him to strike a blow against her in vengeance for the Mary he adored. The Irish fighting seemed to offer him that chance at last but news of the peace in Ireland killed him and David Gordon, skilled swordsman but inexperienced in fighting, continues the journey to Ireland alone. There the story begins and rides on at a magnificent gallop, with David Gordon finding experience in war and in love, making friends and enemies among the English and discovering deep kinship among the Gael. It is a story of hot action and high romance, with the dunt of battle and the clasp of true friendship and the light touch of love thick amongst its pages. There are only two pieces of verse in the whole book but they are magnificent. First, at Dungiven, when Donal Ballagh at last hears the news he has been waiting for of his love Amy, kept under guard by her father in Galway, the old seannachie Tourlough Mac an Teaclan touches his harpstrings to make the soul shiver and sings in a whisper the throat aching, lovely song of Bright Una:

Girl, now that my eyes
Again shall look long on you,
Girl, now that my heart
Is athirst in the drouth for you,
Girl, now that my soul
Yearns deep for the deeps in you,
Now, while my life has a wing,
Do I sing my song to you.

Eyes, deep as the dark of the sky,
Eyes, bright as the sheen of the sea,
Face, pale with the pallor of dreams,
Hair, flame of red bronze breeze free –
I am drowned in your eyes and your dreams,
The flame of your hair is in me.

Girl, if never my eyes
Again might look long on you,
Girl, if ever my heart
Is drained dry for the drouth of you,
Girl, if ever my soul
Is lost for the loss of you,
Still, though my life has no wing,
Will I sing my song to you. [80]

Later, in different mood, David Gordon and a few of his men are trapped inside the walls of Sligo after a night's fierce fighting and driving the Sassenach to the very gates of the town, in a welter and red haze of blows, charge and counter charge. Throughout the long fight he has been cool and cautious, shepherding his troop, but in the face of what looks like certain death he throws off restraint and lets the swordsman in him have free rein, with the long flickering blade of his Andrea Ferrara creating a legend of terror. And he sings gaily as he fights the "Sword Song of Gillian the Black":

I am the Sword – hammered and wrought
　　By Gillian, for Gillian.
Where, now, the swank men, lean men who fought
　　By Gillian, for Gillian?
Dust in the wind, clay in the rain,
　　Like Gillian, ho! Gillian!
Still am I clean, blade without stain –
　　Dead Gillian, dust Gillian! [81]

That is pulse racing poetry.

The whole book is full of incident and yet what makes it so outstanding is the ease of transition from fierce action to beautifully calm description, from riot to romance, from sharp dialogue to easy speculation. The characterisation is superb, from the hero himself David Gordon – and the book is full of heroes English and Irish as well as the Scot – to the nastiest villain Maurice Walsh produced, the brutal Captain Sir William Cosby of Cong. The friendship between David and his cousin Donal is a fine warming one, vividly painted from the moment of first meeting, but the tie between David and the old gentle fighting priest Father Senan is simply beautiful.

If this had been the only book Maurice ever wrote, he could stand on it and call himself a gifted storyteller, yet the next book in the group *And No Quarter* is even better. It is presented as a chronicle of the wars of Montrose as told by Martin Somers, surgeon and adjutant of women in O'Cahan's regiment, and it relates the adventures of

Martin and his foster brother Tadg Mor. There are two strong women, fair and dark, to provide the romance: Margaret Anderson, rescued from the stocks of the kirk in the sack of Aberdeen, and Iseabel Rose, rescued from Ardclach where her own father held her behind a locked door. They are entwined with Martin Somers, whether he likes it or not, in a love story which moves along now slowly, now ftly against the clash of armies and the lightning forays of Montrose's Highland and Irish fighting men. When Meg Anderson is killed amongst the women butchered by Balcarres' horse the grief of the clans is too great to bear. Throughout the book, the writing has a sureness of touch that shows the true craftsman and a conciseness of style that manages to strike the right note in each succeeding passage. That touch is never more clearly in evidence than in the doom-laden, elegaic, throat catching passage that describes the return to camp of Martin and Tadg with the body of Meg.

I took her body on my saddle-bow back to Dunkeld.

We overtook the six women on the road; and Tadg Mor rode behind me, a wounded woman in his arms and one behind him, strapped to his belt. When we came to the margin of the camp the four women with us lifted their voices in the woeful Irish caoine, and Ireland and the Highlands, men and women, swept about us like the waves of the sea. Then did that woeful lament swell and roll against the walls of the hills, and in it pealed the savage note from the throats of the men. It shook all Dunkeld.

Colkitto, bareheaded, came running. Montrose himself galloped on horseback from the manse where he was lodging, his long hair flying behind him. The Irish and Highlandmen stormed round him, and Colkitto, hearing the news, grasped him by the thigh.

"Lead us out now!" Alasdair roared in his great voice. "Lead us out now, Seumas Graham!"

But Montrose struck his hand away, lifted himself in the stirrups and raised a clenched fist in the air. His face had lost all its fresh colour, and his eyes blackened under his black brows.

"The hurt is mine," he cried, and his voice carried across the valley. "The hurt is mine, for Scotsmen did this. I will lead you out and our vengeance shall be full."

And the high maddening Gaelic slogan resounded from all the hills.

That night O'Cahan and fifty horsemen brought in our dead from Methven Wood, and the whole army waked them till the dawn . . . But why do I go on rending my heart? I am crying now as I write.

We buried our dead in the clear pale dawn, and all the pipers marched behind playing the heart-aching "Soiridh: Farewell My Fair One". In Spynie Tower I had promised Margaret that parting tune, and she had it now, though her ears were deaf. And three Irish regiments and ten Highland clans marched behind her; she was wearing her silken gown but it did not swing, and her silver buckled shoon were on her feet; but she rode on no white horse, and she had no silver girdle on the span of her waist.

Kilsyth was the vengeance Montrose led us to.[82]

The discipline of the writing is quite striking. Maurice was always inclined to over-exuberance in his descriptions, carried away sometimes by the richness of his painter's eye but the control in this book is perfect. Maurice himself thought it was his best effort, as did Neil Gunn.

Your movement of masses, of armies, is good. The whole historic treatment is excellent and I can see your whole self shaping up every now and then to assessment and judgement – a thing that is new to you but which you carry off nobly.[83]

One cannot leave *And No Quarter* without mentioning one of the most engaging characters, Ranald Ban MacKinnon of Mull, a Highlander of fierce pride and quick temper, gay, fleering, staunch-hearted, brave and great a talker. At the end of the book Martin Somers promises the tale of Ranald Ban's adventures in Ireland. Alas it never appeared.

Sons of the Swordmaker, which was published in 1938, is a different kind of book altogether. It grew out of a story Maurice wrote for *The Dublin Magazine* in 1923 called "The Woman Without Mercy", about Delgaun, his brother Urnaul and the woman Alor, who drove men to kill. The early story is heavily imbued with the Celtic twilight. By the time Maurice came to rewrite and expand it, however, the whole tone had changed to that of a saga, at one with the strong tales of the Red Branch heroes. Orugh the swordmaker and his five sons – Urnaul who fails to possess the woman Alor, Cond who is killed trying to avenge Urnaul, Flann who loses a hand in a similar attempt, Maur the songmaker and Delgaun the Face of Stone – are set in an epic tale of passion and doom. The language is faintly archaic in style but wholly lyrical.

Baravais is lonely by the marshes of the Rem
With the bittern booming weary and the plover's pain,
The high, keening, shaken whistle of the curlew
Calling rain.

Wandering men of Baravais go many roads from Rem,
Their feet on all the winding ways, keels on plain of sea,
Till the hollow homing hunger strongly murmur
"What seek ye?"

Then homing back to Baravais come weary men of Rem,
To the slope below the pine wood, to the slow, long summer   day,
Till the hollow wander hunger once more whisper
"Come away".[84]

The book falls into two parts, the first being the story of Delgaun and Alor, the second chronicling the adventures of Flann of the one hand and telling the story of the sacking of the hostel of Da Derga. Flann's story is of the very stuff of romance, imbued with fate and fable, mixing high deeds and humour, savagery and sensitivity, with great skill and effect. The book was much in advance of its time, in no way resembling the conventional novel or historical romance. Again, it is the work of a craftsman.

The last book in this group is *Son of Apple* which was written during the war but not published until 1947. It is a delightful story, a rendering of an old folk tale translated from the Irish by Catriona MacLeod but given life and vividness and humour by Maurice Walsh. It is a fairy story of wizards and giants and magic and romance told in a light simple style with vivid and yet delicate descriptions. Maurice had learned to use his rich imagination and gifted tongue to stunning effect. Neil Gunn was much impressed:

> The whole thing was a delight to me. The sonorous tone of your bellowing poet's voice was solemn with laughter and I don't know anyone else who could have brought it off. You brought it off in a way you didn't bring off *Sons of the Swordmaker* which, however good the writing, could not be formally brought off because its whole ethos belonged to another age, difficult in spirit and outlook. For the same reason, no-one can write a ballad today, however fine the poetry they put intillt. The King sat in Dunfermline town drinking the blood red wine once and forever. You cannot get him sitting in Dunfermline toun making linoleum, not anyway with the same outlook. He'd probably need vers libre for linoleum. And a bottle of Bass. *Son of Apple* cheered me to chuckles, as all good drink should. It was like coming on yourself and you knowing you have more than the price of one drink behind you. Begod, it was grand. For you could have come such a helluva cropper.[85]

These four books show Maurice Walsh the storyteller at the peak of his achievement. As historical romances or folklore made real, it is difficult to see how they could be bettered.

The short stories are collected in four books: *Thomasheen James, Man-of-no-Work* (1941), *Son of a Tinker* (1951), *The Honest Fisherman* (1954) and *The Smart Fellow* (1964). Nearly all the stories in these books appeared in magazines, particularly the *Saturday Evening Post* and *Chambers Journal*, before being collected in book form. *Thomasheen James, Man-of-no-Work* contains eleven stories about that unpredictable character based loosely on Tom O'Gorman. Peter O'Donovan suggested the title for the collection. They are amusing colourful pieces and were very popular when they first appeared. In Thomasheen, Maurice created a genuinely amusing and original character. Once created, of course, Thomasheen James grew in his own way and bore less and less resemblance to the original Tom O'Gorman.

Son of a Tinker contains the story of that name and eight others. "The Bonesetter" is the best of them, a swiftly moving story of Ireland in the days of George III and of Garodh O'Connor the bonesetter, captain of France, with a gift of healing that he may not refuse and a deadly sword. Another story in this collection is very fine, "My Fey Lady", which tells of a three-hundred-year-old wrong put right by the faith of a woman sib to the plea from her foremother of old time.

The Honest Fisherman contains six stories, two of them about Thomasheen James. "The Hoplologist" which was originally called "The Sword of Yung-lo" is a variant of the worm turning theme, with a tinge of magic about the sword itself. "Take Your Choice" is also well done, a fairy godmother story where young Sean, offered a young and fair and virtuous lady or twenty thousand pounds, chooses the lady. She makes him a pillar of the community and at the age of sixty plus, with the success of the world around him, he begins to wonder what would have happened to his life and to him if he had made the other choice. He dreams one night that he took the money and went to the devil and when he wakes up in the morning does just that. His story ends at the age of ninety, when he marries his fourth tinker woman and dies in the odour of sanctity.

The Smart Fellow was the collection of seven stories on which Maurice was working when he died. Three are about Thomasheen James and of the rest the best is "The Missing Meerschaum", a hilarious tale of heaven and hell and the vagaries of the keepers of the many different Gates of Heaven.

Finally, in this short review of Maurice Walsh's books, there are the two detective stories, *The Man in Brown* (1945) and *Danger Under the Moon* (1956). Maurice liked reading detective stories, like his father before him, and naturally thought he might try writing them; but it was not really his metier and while the two books are well enough constructed Maurice himself was not very pleased with them. *The*

Man in Brown is a contrived tale although Con Madden, the left-handed detective, is skilfully drawn. *Danger Under the Moon* is better in that the plot is more compact and the action quick and there are some very well drawn cameos in the minor parts, such as the apparently gross but surprisingly agile Superintendent Farley.

First and last Maurice Walsh was a storyteller in a vivid mould. His gift was the ability to make vision and reality coalesce in the mind of his reader, to make the hills and glens breathe and live and to people them with strong, engaging, convincing characters. His dialogues and conversations ring true from the tinker to the earl. His ear was acute for the niceties and peculiarities of speech. Indeed, he used to take issue sometimes with his publishers over corrections to his spellings.

> Your printer is doing good work, only he thinks I am one damn, dam, dom bad speller. I intend those spellings, darn it, depending on context, dialect, pause, stress etc. In fact, I intend all my spellings, except for the few obvious mistakes by the typist, blast her – I mean dem her. [86]

Careful as he was about details of speech it is his prose that reveals how naturally storytelling came to him. He spoke from the heart, from observation and memory. Even his letters have the quality of the skilled storyteller in their construction. one written in 1956 begins: "As I write, thunder is rolling down the stairs of the sky and the rain falling."

He himself said of writing: "It takes a little practice but not much. The secret is proper visualisation – a good sense of sound and colour." [87]

As Maurice's skill with words sharpened and was refined, he evolved a simple direct style that is immediately appealing. He can ramble and reminisce but it is in the manner of an accomplished speaker who seems to digress from his main theme but never loses sight of it. Maurice saw clearly from the beginning of his professional career just how he wanted to write and he succeeded.

> The sluice box chatter of classical English leaves you cold, I hope. A few great ones could pull it off. Pater sometimes, de Quincey often, Winston Churchill not infrequently. But if you want to get the real thrill out of English, hold as close as you can to Anglo Saxon. The Anglo Saxons were a simple people . . . and they were very painstaking in saying what they meant and so had to have many shades of meaning in their words; and we subtle races, the Celts and pre-Celts, found their language a finer medium than our own. That explains everything. [88]

His own style was direct, simple and very effective. The content of his books was essentially wholesome and he had the ability to touch the heartstrings with both sadness and joy. His themes were romantic in a visionary and honourable sense, adventurous in a vivid and exciting way. He made particularly telling use of the return of the native or the arrival of the stranger to precipitate action, as in *The Small Dark Man* or *Trouble in the Glen* or many others. But the action thus set in train would be honourable in intention – and in execution.

The impish, irreverent Maurice would have loved to have written a banned book just for the hell of it, but there was never a possibility of that. Bryan MacMahon put his finger on the essential point about Maurice the author when he said that the image one gets from the book is exactly that of the man himself. There was about the man and his works a sense of wholeness which goes a long way towards accounting for the wide appeal of the stories. The man himself was exceptionally engaging and attractive and the force of his personality shines through his characters. The books themselves have delicacy and understanding, compassion, strength and deep emotion and reflect the author's own experiences of sorrow and of joy. The characters who people the books are richly varied and all vivid and convincing but it was in the descriptions of scene and the building of atmosphere that Maurice's brightest powers showed themselves. His books breathe the open air, the clear, invigorating, mind and soul-clearing air of the Highlands and the west of Ireland. He was not a writer of cities and city people, but of mountain and stream, of hill and plain in Moray and in Kerry. The pages of his books take their strength from the clean outdoors and the high ideals of the people who live and work and play there. Strong, fine, open places with soaring vistas and wide horizons produce people of rare quality. Maurice Walsh was one of them.

The Bust Party
Left to right: Seamus Wilmot, Eugene O'Connor, Nel Broderick,
Maurice Walsh, Gerald Broderick, Peter O'Donovan.

The Bust

Chapter 13. **The Man.**

What sort of man lay behind the storyteller? I hope that a picture has emerged from these pages of someone who managed the difficult feat of preserving throughout his long life a high personal code of integrity and honour, along with a sense of mischief that was never malicious but often outrageous. He was a man who kept his sorrows and disappointments to himself but shared his joys and successes.

Like all strong characters he had some great loves and certain abiding hates. He loved Ireland and Toshon and his family and his friends. He loved Scotland but hated the British Empire (though never the British people). He hated all forms of bigotry and hypocrisy and never hesitated to speak out against those poisonous vices wherever he found them, in Church or State. His one intolerance, his friends used to say, was of intolerance itself. He could not see bigotry and not speak out. "A man that knows is always compelled to use his knowledge," he used to say, "in spite of himself. Always be sure that the man who does nothing is only capable of doing that." In essence he himself was a Christian and a socialist but his faith, though deeply personal, was never unquestioning. He left the Church twice, though he returned to it. Catholicism was a fundamental part of his Irish heritage. "Hibernia semper fidelis" was a fact of life for him and the mild and genial and humanitarian side of Irish Catholicism was bred into him. That is not something easily acquired if one does not start off with it.

I've just read Graham Greene's latest – *Burnt Out Case*. Good, but with a lack, and he has something hidden at the back of his mind, like all converts. English converts to Catholicity don't like Irish Catholics, and reasonably too, for we can't help show contempt for the turncoat. You can't convert a Presbyterian. Toshon was never really converted. You can't convert an Irishman either – he's too pagan behind all. Englishmen, of course, are not worth converting. I mean, it doesn't pay, they are too wise, or prudent or something.[89]

Maurice's God was a gentle deity and his heaven was not an exclusive place. Men and women of integrity of any religion would be accepted gladly. In one of his poems, which he never entirely finished to his satisfaction, he muses on a kind of heaven, a house of healing, a place of dreams where the broken men of old might be renewed and made whole again.

And Christ the Son of God and man
  in the gloaming sits Him down

Among these men of virtue
    and dubious renown.
While Judas sad, no traitor now
    doth touch His garment hem
And tell us there his old mad dream
    of a new Jerusalem.
And Lucifer, that great dark one
    would sit at Christ His knee,
Whose broken hand rests on his hair
    for all the world to see;
For if men hold that Christ came down
    to save both me and you,
Then by the quenched fires of Hell,
    He saved the Devil too.[90]

That is a characteristic Walsh notion. Even the Devil had some good in him and might be let into Maurice's heaven, but bigots of all kinds would be kept out. In his book *And No Quarter* he put something of the strength of that conviction into his denunciation of the Covenanters who massacred in the name of Christ.

I have said many hard and bitter things against the Solemn League and Covenant, but let no-one hold that I am against the Scottish Kirk when I say that the Solemn League and Covenant was the most bowelless, Christianless institution that ever shackled Scotland in the name of religion, and Scotland has been sorely shackled three or four times. I am myself Episcopalian, though not a Roman, but I do believe that the National Convenant, renewed and proclaimed seven years before the time of which I am writing, was a very necessary weapon to save the religion and freedom of Scotland from the episcopal follies of the first Charles. And I maintain that the rebirth of that Covenant twenty years later in the persecuting time of the second Charles was a noble one, and gave the blood of the martyrs for the rights of reason and tolerance. But I also hold that the body of ministers and lairds that ruled Scotland in the name of the Solemn League and Covenant during the wars of the Parliament was the most tyrannical body in all Christendom before or since – and there have been many tyrannies in Christendom. It was a theocracy whose real aim was power; the god it fulminated was a Jehovah more terrible than any mad Jahveh ever conjured up in the mad dreams of the maddest prophet of Israel. It humiliated noble men, set its heel on the helpless, butchered women, tortured prisoners, slew honest fighting men surrendered under quarter, broke its bond, sold its king, sold its country, bartered its conscience; and Cromwell, whom it helped to make supreme, crushed it into fragments under his own firmer heel as something too abominably intolerant for that most intolerant age.[91]

That was strong stuff from Martin Somers of O'Cahan's Regiment, but it was also Maurice Walsh saying what he thought, in a heartfelt way. The interesting thing about Maurice Walsh's attacks, however, like this one or the criticism of the Northern Ireland clique in "Ireland in a Warring Europe", is that they are always directed against factions, or governments or groups, never against individual people. Maurice believed that mobs (whether organised in governments or parties or just crowds) caused trouble. Individual people might go astray but could be helped back to sanity. He hated to hear ill spoken of anyone, however merited, and did not do it himself. That was one of the strongest characteristics of this warm, friendly, likeable man.

Those who knew him are unanimous in their praise, so uniform in their judgement in fact that a seed of doubt creeps in. No one could be such a paragon, one thinks. The man must have had some faults. And yet, probe as one will, through conversation and enquiry or through letters and the dusty accumulation of paper that forms the audit trail of a long life, the picture never wavers. There was no vice in him.

Certainly he had flaws. He was stubborn, argumentative, teasing and rash in the extreme with money. But he was kindly to a fault and the softest of touches for the itinerants who called regularly at his door, sure of largesse. Whenever he sold a story or a book he would distribute some of the proceeds, not just to his immediate family but pretty far afield. He never made any fuss about it or told anyone what he was doing but simply sent out a few cheques. It was inevitable that he would be taken advantage of. He guaranteed loans and lost his money time and again throughout his life. As late as 1962 when he was eighty-three years old and should have learned his lesson, a good friend let him in for £1,500 and he paid up without a word of recrimination. The sons and daughters and friends of his friends took his books and his money and never returned them, but he would have been the last person to have mentioned it, hurt though he was. It was not as if he were shy or retiring: far from it. He always spoke up for what he believed in and said straight out to anyone's face what he thought on an issue of principle, but in terms of personal relations he tended to overlook faults and concentrate on virtues. It was all part of his basic belief and trust in good fellowship.

If there is a key to the complex Walsh personality, that is where one finds it. Good fellowship was the theme of his life from his early days in Kerry, through the golden years of the Excise Service and to the last years. Friendship was not a casual thing for him though he had casual friends in plenty. Friendship for Maurice was a relationship in which one man looked on another with respect and admiration and trust and love. A friend, a real friend, was sib, kin in thought and blood and bone though no blood relationship might exist. Friendship of that sort usually came in the first glance or not at all but once established was never to be broken. Friends were to be supported and cherished even though their friends and their families might not come up to the same standard.

A man with a vision like that was bound to be hurt but the vision itself never dimmed and it infected those who knew him. I remember the look of incredulity on the face of John B. Keane, the Listowel writer, when I asked him what people in Kerry thought of Maurice Walsh fifteen years after his death.

"He's loved here," he said. "Loved."

Bryan MacMahon speaks of him with similar affection as an extraordinarily gentle and generous man and stresses that the image one gets of him from his books was exactly the sort of man he was: "neat, graceful, gentle, courteous, honourable – old fashioned, if you like." Both of those men have the gift of words themselves but much as they admired Maurice Walsh the writer it was the man they loved.

What was it about Maurice Walsh that attracted so much affection? He was generous, but so are many people. He had a friendly manner, a twinkling eye and a good memory for names and faces, which are endearing qualities, but not unique ones. What gave him power, I think, was his integrity, the deeply rooted sense of personal honour which he himself tried to live up to and which he expected to find in others. That was what his idea of "good fellowship" was about. And, expecting to find it, find it he did. Honour and integrity are infectious if you really believe in them.

Maurice believed in people. Of course there were times when he was disillusioned but he always picked up again. He put it perfectly in his first book.

"We always went to the fight and we always fell. We fail because we aim so high, but sometimes we gain what we do not be expecting."

"And what we do not want."

"And that too. I will now play for you the lament that John Lom played for the loss of Inverlochy."

He played for me that tune, pacing slowly up and down on the stone flags – a tune of failure and defeat, and yet full of a terrible, high, unconquerable spirit: the spirit of the singer, proud of his great singing, and knowing that his song is a supreme call to the spirit of the defeated.

" 'Tis a queer race we are," said Quinn. "The songs we make are more important than the loss or love we sing of. 'Mavrone, Mavrone, bitter was the blow,' we sing. But, Christ God! what a splendid fine song we are making of it. I will now play you an old air called 'To Cashel I Am Going.'

He played that tune – a fast air with a cry in it:

'Tis a pity I came where my name
Was unknown in the town,
Where no-one could tell how so well
I had earned renown.
Then the young one I sought would have thought
Herself honoured in knowing
A man of my name and good fame –
So to Cashel I'm going.

There friends I will meet in the street,
And we'll drink the red wine
That came o'er the main out of Spain
To cheer hearts like mine.
And no-one I'll tell what a hell
I always am knowing
When I think of a face in this place –
So to Cashel I'm going.

"This is a jig tune," said Quinn, "and it is a lament as well, for the man that made it took sorrow with him in his going. But he had a great, naive, proud spirit, and at Cashel he was a man amongst men. We always went to the fight, says the old word, and we always fell. But we always go, and we will keep on going, Tom King – when it is required of us."

My friend had the right word for me always. [92]

That was Tom King and Neil Quinn in the book, Maurice Walsh and Neil Gunn in real life. The passage says a lot about both the fictional and the real characters. All four were staunch, true, leal men, of the highest honour. They represented the ideal made real and the real made ideal.

In addition to a strong sense of personal integrity Maurice Walsh had tremendous compassion, an awareness of and understanding for the frailty of human kind, a sympathy for the difficulties of others in living up to a high personal code. That is a very unusual combination. It is a rare human being who can set himself high standards, with humility and honour and humour, and yet treat with kindness and understanding those of his brethren who cannot do the same. What was important was to keep trying – we always went to the fight and we always fell. In another man that might be a counsel of gloom but in Maurice it was an affirmation of faith.

He was a humble man who achieved great fame in his life-time and saw it wane but never lost the capacity to laugh at himself. He consistently underrated his own ability. When asked about his writing he would pass it off as "yarns" or recount with great amusement how he would occasionally write essays for his grandson Maurice when the young man was at Blackrock College and never get better than seven out of nine!

Most of the present memories of Maurice Walsh in Ireland and elsewhere relate to the last period of his life, the twenty years from the middle 1940s to his death in 1964. On the whole it was a pleasant time for him after the war when the world began to settle down again, but of course life had changed in Ireland as elsewhere. Maurice Walsh's stories and style were now somewhat old-fashioned. Honour and dignity and fidelity in fictional characters were no longer the standards to which heroes and heroines were supposed to reach, any more than they were then the standards in real life. Qualities like those were a little like good clothes that have gone shabby, to be used where they could be but discarded if they could not.

Maurice continued to write – by then it was as natural as breathing to have something in preparation for publication – but his output slowed down and he wrote mainly stories for magazines and for collection into books rather than full-length novels. That was partly because he was getting older and slowing down a bit, but more because of a growing disillusionment with the world and its rabid inhabitants. He was not gloomy or depressed in his everyday life, far from it, but there is in his letters a growing wistfulness for the old days and faces. In the quiet moments when he sat at his desk weaving words he must have wondered if the world could ever again see through unclouded eyes the high bright hills and glens peopled with men and women of honour and probity and salty quiet humour that he himself still remembered so warmly and so well. He had called *The Spanish Lady* the "last squeeze of the bag" but with *Castle Gillian* in 1948 and *Trouble in the Glen* in 1950 he managed to wring a sizeable volume of romance from an allegedly dried up source. Of course, he had the *Castle Gillian* plot in his head anyway, but the plot is a small thing compared to the prose and characterisation, which are in the old romantic style. What happpened in short is that his natural resilience and belief in the essential goodness of humanity came to the fore again so that he could be optimistic once more.

The family helped, as always. He used to walk his grandson to school each morning and wander down to meet him at lunchtime. His son Ian, who had married again, came home from the war with his wife Patricia. He had decided to stay in the RAMC so the visit was in the nature of a leave, but a joyous one. Maurice had taken to Patricia right away and gave her a copy of his book *Green Rushes* inscribed "To Patricia, who once was green, the cratur". (Patricia's maiden name had been Green.) On that trip Patricia had brought some of the first nylon underthings that were then coming on the market. She had washed them and hung them out to dry when it started to rain. Thomasheen James brought them in, all crushed up in one hand. Maurice looked at them and shook his head. "Once upon a time," he said, "you didn't know what you were getting until you unwrapped it."

Neil too came home from the war. He had gone into the RAMC after he qualified. He had married in 1943 and his wife was called Máirín, like his brother Maurice's wife. They had to be distinguished in correspondence about the family as Máirín Maurice and Máirín Neil, which worked well. Máirín Neil typed the first draft of *The Spanish Lady* and Maurice Walsh paid her the full professional rate for the job, in cash. It was the first money she had earned so she took Neil to Jammet's restaurant and blew the lot. There was a party at Ard Na Glaise two nights before the wedding with about fifty people. Maurice enjoyed himself hugely. "Everyone drank what they wanted and when they wanted and then when they didn't want. I was as sober as a thrice filled sherry cask."[93]

Maurice was in fact trying to move from Ard Na Glaise at that time because it was much too big for himself, his grandson and a house-keeper – and Thomasheen when he was around. He nearly bought a smaller place near his son Maurice in 1943 but missed it. In the end it was 1950 before he moved to a new house nearby called Green Rushes, where his grandson Maurice and his family live still. His son Maurice moved into Ard Na Glaise. There was no summerhouse at Green Rushes but Maurice converted the garage into a study. A car was pointless after Toshon died and young Maurice was too young to drive. Thomasheen moved with them of course and Maurice built on a room at the back for him, a wooden hut that suited him fine.

Thomasheen still took off without warning when the mood took him but when he was around he would light the fires and do the shopping. Maurice's sister Bridget, who was keeping house for them at that time, ruled the hapless Tom with a rod of iron. She never trusted him in the way that Maurice did. Tom's needs were small, though: the shed to lay his head down, a few old clothes, a bite to eat and enough cash to go to Boland's for a pint each night. He used to be in the bar of an evening, telling outrageous stories of the shocking tyranny of Bridget (Bridgie) or of Maurice himself to anyone who would listen or buy him a drink. As often as not it was the author himself who was listening gleefully through in the kitchen or, in later and more modernised years, the lounge. Tom would eventually come roaring home to the stables at Ard Na Glaise or his shed at Green Rushes, stamping and growling and making a great din. All Maurice's friends knew him and took no notice, but eventually Maurice would go to the window and shout, "Thomasheen! Shut up out of that!"

There would be a few more curses and some more clattering and banging but then Tom would subside into silence. He was a completely free agent but knew where to draw the line.

There was a time in the late 1950s though when Tom fell in with a shyster who told him that he had grounds for an action against the author of the Thomasheen James stories on grounds of defamation of character. Tom came home tanked up one night, determined to make his claim. Maurice laughed at the cheek of it but Tom had the bit between his teeth and threatened to sue Maurice for his "rights". He became overwrought and shouted and swore and actually took a swing at Maurice in his rage. Maurice was nearly eighty then and Thomasheen a little younger but Maurice waved the blow aside and struck the boiling Tom once, on the chest. It was the old devastating body blow and it did the trick. Thomasheen collapsed and that was the end of that.

Tom had been growing steadily more erratic as the years went by. He agreed to go into a mental hospital for a bit but discharged himself and disappeared. He came to the house demanding his "papers", for all the world like the tramp in Harold Pinter's play *The Caretaker*, but of course Thomasheen never had a "paper" in his life. In any case he did not know that Maurice was dying and in fact the funeral cortège passed him in the street without his knowing it. Maurice would have hated that. Thomasheen simply disappeared.

But in 1950 all that was still fourteen years ahead and those years were pleasant ones. As he grew older Maurice's life became more leisurely and more predictable. He got up later in the mornings, having had breakfast and read the papers in bed. He would work for the rest of the morning in his study if he felt like it or write letters to his relatives and friends if he did not. The afternoons were for going out or being visited and the evenings were for Boland's. Most of the old crowd were still about: Peter O'Donovan and his wife Ethel, Jack and Lily Spears, Humphrey Kerins, Eugene O'Connor, Dan Healy, Gerald and Nel Broderick and others. Peter Flynn, a Dublin solicitor, and his wife Maeve were friends of the Brodericks and therefore friends of Maurice, at one remove as it were. The two ladies used to do crossword puzzles with Maurice regularly on Wednesday afternoons. It was Nel who said of Green Rushes that it was a house where it always seemed to be afternoon, with people drinking and talking and laughing.

Friday night was open night with plenty to drink and a big cold roast. The visitor got a fork and bread and butter and then had to help himself to whatever he wanted. There still had to be a visit to Boland's, especially if any of the visitors had not been before. The women in the family, his sisters and daughters-in-law and nieces, tended to disapprove of Boland's but without the slightest effect. It was a must. Bryan MacMahon remembers one hilarious evening there, after his play *Bugle in the Blood* was first put on at the Abbey, when a friend of Maurice's from Kerry, Tim Cotter, vanquished the Dublin literati in argument, much to Maurice's delight. One up for Kerry.

Usually someone would call for him and take him to Boland's and back and in later years his grandson Maurice used to do it. Occasionally he would be too busy or involved to notice the time and his grandfather would look pointedly at the clock a few times and then say, "Well, if you won't bring me, I'll bloody well walk!"

Saturday was always a good day. His friend Paddy Lynch, who was in the tweed business in Dublin, would arrive on the twelve o'clock bus which used to stop very conveniently outside Boland's. Maurice used to meet him there and the pair of them would return happily to the house about one thirty for lunch, which was invariably corned beef, cabbage and potatoes, a great favourite and a tradition no one would dare to break. After lunch they would retire to the study for a talk, in which Paddy's snores were much the louder. Saturday night remained Excise night, as always.

He was often back in Kerry, of course, and always tried to get down at the end of September for Listowel Race Week. All the tinkers would gather round him and remind him that he had written about them in his books. Of course he gave them all something. He bet on every race but seldom won. Gambling as such never interested him, even the cut-throat Irish card game Spoil Five he mentions in his books, although he did play from time to time.

It was a great delight to him to take his close friends down to Kerry and show them the fabulous scenery of the Ring. He even liked to show it to the natives. In 1956 he and Seamus Wilmot made a memorable tour of the Ring of Kerry together and were lost sight of for days. Even at eighty-four, he made the tour with his daughter-in-law Máirín Maurice, and his niece Dorothy and her husband Andrew Melvin. Maurice was a small man but very distinguished with his white hair and beard, bright twinkling eyes and tweed cloak and hat. The cloak was particularly distinctive, with a lining of Wallace tartan. On that tour in 1963 Andrew Melvin remembers the warmth with which Maurice was received everywhere. They stopped at many a pub and in each one the publican would come forward joyfully:

"Is it yourself, Mossie?"

"It is."

"Are you well, Lord love you? Come in."

And of course the welcome would be extended to his friends while people in the bar would nudge one another and say, "Look! 'Tis himself."

He was recognised everywhere he went, in Kerry or Dublin itself, with great affection. In Kerry the tweed hat took on an identity of its own: "That's a fine Maurice Walsh hat you've got."

Maurice was out in all weathers in his cloak and hat, disdaining the use of an umbrella. He paid for it often with colds and 'flu. One day, when he was about to leave Green Rushes in torrential rain his sister Jule (Julia), who was looking after him for a bit at that time, tried to get him to take an umbrella which someone had left at the house. He recoiled at the idea. "I wouldn't be *seen* with it!" he said. What Maurice had really wanted was an Irish war cloak with a hood, but he wore the tweed cloak and grew fond of it.

In Kerry his brother Paddy was still at Ballydonoghue and on his visits home Maurice liked to see his old friends there, either in the farmhouse or in O'Sullivan's bar, where he would hold court and eat dishes of mushrooms and periwinkles. People today still remember him at the market in Listowel, moving happily through the bustle of the fair like the best and most democratic of royalty, calling to old friends and stopping for a chat. He had a prodigious memory for names and faces.

"Aren't you Tom?" he would say to a young farmer whose father he had known years before.

"I am," the young man would reply, blushing happily to be recognised.

"Is it pigs you're selling today? What are they fetching now?"

And so on. He had a remarkable capacity for putting people at ease, wherever he was, in town or country, farmhouse or conference room. There was an aura of friendliness and warmth about him that young people in particular found attractive. With his white hair and beard and twinkling eyes he looked like a friendly man even before he spoke.

He grew his beard first after a bout of 'flu and it suited him. A well-to-do Listowel widow who had had her eye on him for some time stopped him one day in the Square and said, "Oh, Maurice, why did you let that dreadful beard grow?"

"To keep away designing widows," he said, but smiled.

He shaved it off after a time but his sons persuaded him to let it grow again. After about the seventh day he met Nel Broderick in Grafton Street in Dublin and pulled his collar up around his face in an exaggerated gesture and made as if to hide from her. Nel took it seriously though and thought he had been on the bottle. She gave him hell, told him he should be ashamed and insisted that he take a taxi right home, have a bath and go to bed.

"Yes, Nel, I will," he said meekly and roared with laughter all the way home.

Of course, he was a tremendous boost to local writers in Kerry such as Seamus Wilmot, who brought him a story to read in 1922 and was a close friend all his life, or John B. Keane or Bryan MacMahon. He was always ready to help and encourage. Bryan MacMahon relates that when he showed Maurice a very early story Maurice read it and said that he should put it aside for a while and come back to it after trying some more writing, serving his apprenticeship, as it were. In particular he ought to "beware of sheer shining". That was his way of telling the young MacMahon very gently and kindly that his story was not up to scratch, as Bryan readily admits it was not. He was a bit cast down at the time though and Maurice took pains to encourage him in his own typically modest way.

"Look," he said, "if John Walsh's son of Ballydonoghue can do it, so can you."

It is impossible to overemphasise how much Kerry and its people meant to Maurice Walsh. On his very last visit, the year before he died, he walked all round the farm at Ballydonoghue on his own, a thing he had not done for years. It was a farewell and folk there knew it.

In Dublin too he had a lot of friends and saw them often. They were always at some ploy or other and it was the excisemen, active or retired, who were usually in the thick of it. Naturally, much of the activity centred round drink. Dan Healy, Gerald Broderick and Maurice started importing cases of French and German wine. Maurice used to pour a glass of wine for Dan and ask his opinion of it, especially if he knew the arrival of others was imminent. He would pour nothing for himself, but sit and watch Dan trying to think of something original to say. (Dan used to write about alcohol.) Then Eugene O'Connor or Peter O'Donovan would arrive.

"Well, Eugene, Dan is drinking wine so it's no good offering him a dram but yourself and myself will try a drop."

Dan was a generous man and a great fisherman who each season sent Maurice the first salmon he caught, wrapped in leaves.

With so much neat spirit available the Excise coterie was bound to try to do something with it. Maurice had several attempts at making liqueur. The earliest attempt was at St Michael's, with Paddy Lynch, Jack Speirs, Finton Lawlor and Dan O'Donoghue to try the result. His son Maurice was there too, playing the ukelele. Dan O'Donoghue hit the gatepost as he tried to drive home.

On a much later occasion at Green Rushes, Maurice and Dan Healy were deputed to have another go. Maurice had a three gallon stone jar and Dan wrote about wine, so they were obviously well qualified. A couple of gallons of spirit were obtained, but that was the easy part. What about the flavouring? All sorts of forays were then made by the pair up into the hills. They spent days wandering about to return with a handful of sloes or a few herbs. The great night came when they were ready to start, or "compovent" as Maurice used to say, from the old chemists' signs where "compound" was spelled "compovnd". They had flowers and peppermint essence and a multitude of bits ready to try. Dan sat in a chair with the jar on the floor in front of him while Maurice solemnly poured in the alcohol and crushed a few sloes and stirred up the mixture.

"Now, Dan. Try that."

"Mmm. A few more sloes, maybe."

"What about that, now?"

"Well, maybe some more peppermint."

And so it went till Dan pronounced the brew perfect. Maurice was delighted.

"Well, we're away to Boland's."

Dan was willing enough, but his legs were not.

On another occasion Maurice and Gerald Broderick thought of using alcohol as a base for their own aftershave. It came out all right but it was clear and Maurice wanted his coloured. So he put some Angostura bitters in it. It worked fine. He used it all himself and had the most distinctive smell of any man in Dublin.

There was a lot of theorising amongst the crowd about how easy it was to produce the good things in life and Maurice decided to have a go at smoking bacon. He used to get a lot of home-cured bacon up from Kerry so he took a piece of that and salted it solid. Then he got oak chippings and sawdust so as to smoke it, thus removing any possible objection anyone could have to the vile green stuff. Then he pierced an oil drum and hung the fifteen pound flitch over it in the lavatory at Green Rushes. He left it there smoking a whole day, though the flames were licking at it and the thing was half cooked as well as heavily smoked. Maurice would never admit that it was not just right and ate the lot himself. No one else would look at it.

Then there was the tobacco growing episode. For about a year Maurice and his friends grew and cured their own tobacco and professed to like it, though in fact it was not very good and had to be mixed with commercial stuff. Maurice tried rolling a few cigars too and tried them on Paddy Lynch. One was a trick, with the leaf folded over inside so that it would not draw at all.

There was still quite a lot of coming and going of Scottish friends and relatives. Neil and Daisy Gunn were over in 1956 and Maurice went over to Scotland in 1957 for the opening of his friend Father Michael McNicholas's new chapel in Paisley. Of course, he took the opportunity to look up old friends and places, but the old faces were slowly disappearing. The return sea crossing was an interesting one.

> The sea was like a pond and yet an ancient man from Dundee who wanted to see Ireland and had never been to sea afore got squeamish, so I cured him with a small shot of malt whisky and took a mouthful myself as a prophylactic. He got squeamish again but he got no more whisky and thought better of it.[94]

The year 1957 was also the year of his sister Sister Gabriel's golden jubilee as a nun and of course he was down in Kerry for that.

One of the regular highlights of the early post-war years was the ritual that became know as "collecting the pension". Each month Maurice and whoever was about at the time would go into Dublin on the bus to cash his pension cheque. There was not the slightest need to do so but nevertheless into Dublin the party would go to cash the pension and have a quick lunch at Jammet's restaurant.

"We'll have wan dish at Jammet's now," Maurice would say. "Just wan dish."

Jammet's, which is alas no more, was then the best restaurant in Dublin. Anyway, off the party would go. Usually it was a male affair but occasionally the women were allowed along if they were good, particularly in the later years. In the full-blooded version, though, in the late 1940s and early 1950s, the first stop would be at the National City Bank, where Maurice's eldest son Maurice worked, to lodge the cheque. Maurice himself had to come out to witness the operation. Then a large wink to son Maurice and out the party would go, not across Dame Street to Jammet's, as the uninitiated might suspect, but to a bar called the Bodega for two drinks, the second for son Maurice who would arrive shortly afterwards leaving much hilarity behind at the bank where they knew he would be gone for some time. The next step was into Jammet's for "wan dish" upstairs in the Grill. Paddy, the "French" waiter, was in charge and he knew the drill well. When they were all seated, Maurice would look round at Paddy and say, "Paddy, I suppose we could give them a starter, do you think?"

"Well, Mr Walsh, I suppose we could."

And of course it would be a full meal, with a sweet and a bottle of something good. Paddy used to call kebabs by his own name for them, which was "lecabs". On pension day he always had a big table reserved and kept it after lunch because there was a good chance Maurice would be back in the evening. The ritual was that after lunch at Jammet's, Maurice would go off to see Peter O'Donovan for a chat and maybe sample some malt and then go to the Palace Bar, which was Dublin's literary pub at that time. In there he would see people like the editor of *The Irish Times*, or Brendan Behan or Jerome Connor. He might be there long enough but after a few hours, as like as not, the cry would go up: "Wan dish at Jammet's!"

And off they would go, maybe just Maurice's own group, maybe a pubful. But the evening did not end there. When at last it was time to go home off they would go, probably on the bus still, and after leaving the bus the short walk home took them past Eugene O'Connor's door. Only they never did pass it. Nothing was pre-arranged or even mentioned during the day but Maurice never passed the door. In they would go with a bottle of whiskey acquired somewhere along the way and they might be there until two or three in the morning. That was "collecting the pension". In later years Maurice had not quite the stamina for the full ritual and for him it was likely to be just one dish in fact as well as in theory, but everyone with him would be pressed to at least three courses. Máirín Maurice once surprised Paddy, the waiter, when offered the sweet trolley, by asking for chocolate biscuits; Paddy did not have any. On another occasion Maurice took a well known singer called Delia Murphy to Jammet's and encouraged her to try every one of the hors d'oeuvres on offer. He loved enthusiastic excess of that innocent kind.

Through all that social activity he was still writing. After *Trouble in the Glen* in 1950 he produced a collection of stories in 1951 under the title *Son of a Tinker*. All had appeared before in the *Saturday Evening Post* or elsewhere except for a little piece called "Heather Wine", about how the secret of that ancient Gaelic drink had been lost. He got the idea from Neil Gunn, more than likely, for he opens with a typical gesture: "Steady now, steady! Follow your hand, Mr Gunn! But manalive, leave room for a small drop of water."

In 1952 he turned the piece to good account when Desmond Williams, of the firm that made the liqueur Irish Mist, asked him for a piece to help market the drink in the United States. "Heather Wine" was ideal and Maurice turned it into "The Secret of the O'Donchu" for an Irish Mist advertising leaflet.

Another collection of stories, *The Honest Fisherman*, appeared that same year, this time with some new material. Then in 1953 he wrote a series of four articles on whiskey for the *Irish Press*. There could have been few better qualified to do it. Maurice himself had a famous nose for whisky or whiskey, though he himself gave the edge to Neil Gunn:

" . . . the best judge o' good whiskey in four counties, I only knew one better – a writer chap he was, but otherwise fair enough."[95]

Maurice once told his publishers[96] that there were four great Irish whiskies and six Scotch ones. The four Irish were (in 1924):

John Jameson Three Star
John Powers Three Swallows
DWD Fifteen Years Old
Paddy Flaherty.

Unfortunately he did not list the Scotch but Talisker was certainly one of them. At Green Rushes in the later years he had a two gallon stone jar of Powers delivered at frequent intervals, insisting that it come from the "baby" vat. He still kept his own personal measure, a "tailor", which is one-fifteenth of a bottle. Irish measures are generous anyway by United Kingdom standards but the tailor is even more so. Even miniatures are bigger, the naggin being a handy size to slip in a pocket and still a good drink. Maurice's friend Humphrey Kerins used to put one in his pocket after a hard night as a provision against a sore head the next morning. When he got home he would look for a clever hiding place and invariably decided on the base of a big grandfather clock in the hall. He would kneel down carefully and reach into the depths with the naggin. In the harsh light of morning he always forgot where he had hidden it. When the clock was eventually moved, thirty-seven naggins of good Irish were found in the base. Maurice used the story in *The Man in Brown*.

The *Saturday Evening Post* was still glad to use his stories when he cared to send them. There were one in 1951, two in 1953 and no more until the last two in 1961. His work appeared in other magazines too, of course. Foreign interest in his books continued. Danish Book Club editions of *Green Rushes* and *Trouble in the Glen* came out in 1953 and 1954 and that later year saw the publication of the novelised play *A Strange Woman's Daughter*. The last two books were *Danger Under the Moon*, his second detective story, in 1956 and a collection of stories under the title *The Smart Fellow* which came out posthumously in 1964.

He was reading much more than writing by this time: mysticism, philosophy, thrillers and some novels. His comments are perceptive. Of Hemingway's *For Whom the Bell Tolls*, for example, he said that it was:

. . . good, but too sudden in love making . . . Hemingway is a good man to write but he has had to nurture a sense of humour from a weakling plant – even now you cannot be sure whether he means to be witty or humorous or comic or sardonic. But you will have noticed that many of the very great writers are short of humour.[97]

He was very impressed with *Death in the Afternoon*.

In the 1940s he read a lot of foreign novels in translation but was not very happy with that. The only great work to carry something of the original into translation, he thought, was Hugo's *Les Miserables*.

Dr Zhivago did not impress him much: "Not a great book. He was never more than a Christian mystic and the Nobel prize people merely used it as a stick to beat a dog with."[98]

He enjoyed Josephine Tey's books for a while but went off her in the end.

> I've read most of Josephine Tey, but she wrote herself out in the end – and made fun of Hugh McDiarmid. *The Franchise Affair* was her best . . . She gave hell to the Covenanters. She even compared them to the Irish, about whom she knew dam' all. Mind you, Calvinism (or Knoxism) was a hell of a religion – and still is maybe. A religion for righteous men – not a woman's religion at all. Roman Catholicism is the women's religion; it allows' em to fall seven times a day and picks 'em up again.[99]

Maurice himself was a Christian socialist but his irreverence, like his nationalism, remained undimmed. He used to call himself a communist in order to shock his sister Bridget who had very narrow Catholic views, and once called a black retriever dog he had "Bolshie".

A major event occured in 1958, on his seventy-ninth birthday, when he was presented with a bust of his head in bronze, commissioned from the Cork sculptor Seamus Murphy by Maurice's friends. The principal organiser was Peter O'Donovan, himself retired by that time, and the presentation was made at a huge party attended by his family and many friends. The bust was exhibited at the Royal Irish Academy that year and Liam Morrissey wrote an ode to it for *Irisleabhair*. Maurice himself did not like it very much and thought it a bit morbid.

In the following year, his sister Bridget died at the age of eighty-two and he went down to Kerry for the funeral. At that time he was eighty years old himself and, looking at his brothers and sisters, he was happy to see that there were still six out of the original clutch of ten. Lily had died at the age of three and two others in infancy, but Tim was the only one to die as a youngish adult. At that time Sister Gabriel was seventy-six, Paddy seventy-four, Mary seventy-two, Mick seventy and Jule the baby only sixty-seven.

In 1959 he was even thinking of going over to Scotland for the Edinburgh Festival but his health was not good enough. He watched the proceedings from afar with lively interest, though.

> This was a good year for your famous Edinburgh Festival. Though, mind you, "Festival" coupled with "Edinburgh" is rather

a contradiction in terms. Whatever else Edinburgh is, it isn't festive – except it be a feast of reason (mostly false) and a flow of soul (not worth saving). Compton Mackenzie says our Wexford Festival is the real thing. It lasts 144 hours and makes no distinction between day and night – and that's a festival.[100]

Of course he was simply teasing and in fact had a great admiration for the festival and in particular for the imaginative leap that brought it into being when the rest of the United Kingdom was sunk in post-war gloom.

At eighty it was not surprising that his health was less robust than it had been but he was in fact remarkably vigorous. In 1960, though, he had to have prostate treatment. He himself was very matter of fact about it although it worried his family.

You've heard of the prostate gland? It is of biological significance and common to both sexes, but more noticeable in its symptoms in the male. If it withers away, so does the owner. In a man's later years, it is inclined to enlarge and if it does not enlarge too much a man retains his virility and attractiveness. If it enlarges too much, it stops the waterworks and a reasonable operation is required.[101]

He recovered quickly and well. When he was visited in hospital by the family, though, he looked serious and said solemnly, "I'm fine but there is one thing I must not have."

It had come at last. The family looked at each other aghast. No more of the hard stuff? No more Boland's? It had to be faced, though.

"Well, what's that, Dad?" they said.

Maurice paused dramatically and then roared with laughter. "Milk!" he shouted. It was like a reprieve.

He was getting a bit deaf and sometimes wore a hearing aid, especially in public houses where the varying noise level made hearing more difficult. He himself said that he wore it in bars like the gillie that never wore a deerstalker hat after the accident, the accident being that his boss asked him to have a drink and he never heard him.

The year of the operation, 1960, was the year his son Ian went to Jamaica to head the RAMC unit in the West Indies. Maurice was keenly interested in this move to an area that was new to him as well as to his son.

Did Ian tell you of his great air trip over the eight island groups of his bailiwick and the easy going, friendly natives, 98% black, many with Highland and Irish names – relic of penal days. He met a Walsh who claimed kinship – black as a boot and incest his favourite avocation – so race will tell.[102]

Maurice lived a lot through his letters in those last years, keeping in touch with his folk in Scotland and in America. He felt himself getting old and in a merry company, surrounded by laughter and discussion, he would suddenly feel himself a million miles away. But he was still working, on the stories for *The Smart Fellow* and other ideas. He was considering a reissue of some of the material in *While Rivers Run* and *The Road to Nowhere* about Paddy Joe Long for the Canadian market, under a title like *Paddy Joe Talks*, though nothing came of that in the end. Maurice and Máirín were keeping a close eye on him, as was his grandson Maurice and his wife Pauline, for he was certainly ailing. Sharp, though:

> I've got a touch of sciatica, my seasonal complaint, and am avoiding Bolands for a week because whiskey ain't good for it. Still, Maurice comes over and a drop in his pocket. The grouse season nearly killed him – twenty miles for a brace and I only got half a tough one.[103]

During the autumn and winter of that year he went into a decline very rapidly with carcinoma of the left lung and died peacefully at Ard Na Glaise, where his son Maurice then lived, on 18 February 1964.

Both as a writer and as a man Maurice Walsh left a sparkling heritage of words and memories. He himself lived up to his ideals all his days and he achieved his own great toast – health and long life and death in the Ireland he loved. It is a fitting note to end on.

Sláinte gu'saol fada chugat agus bás in Éirinn!

Postscript. **20 February 1964.**

The day was cold and raw but the funeral was a massive affair, to mark the passing of a grand old man of Irish letters. President de Valera came to the mass, which was celebrated by the Rev F. J. Kenny, and the funeral cortège was accompanied by a motorcycle escort across Dublin from St John the Baptist church at Blackrock to Esker cemetery at Lucan. Maurice's sons were there of course and his two sisters Mary and Julia, his brothers Paddy and Mick and a host of friends. He was buried in his famous tweed cloak.

The stone at Esker is a simple one, with the message:

Maurice Walsh

Author

Born Co Kerry 1879, Died Dublin 1964

with him lie his wife

Caroline 1886 - 1940

and his daughter

Elizabeth died 1932

aged three months.

Rest in Peace.

The press carried lengthy and musing tributes, many written by heartbroken close friends. A very much loved Irishman had passed on and the world did seem changed.

The last word on that day rested with Maurice's grandson Ian. Maurice himself would have been the first to urge laughter rather than grief, fond and happy remembrance rather than present sorrow. Back at Ard Na Glaise there was an enormous crush of people and Maurice's son Ian decided that it would ease things a bit if he took a group, consisting of his wife Patricia and his son and daughter-in-law Maurice and Pauline, and his brother Neil off for lunch somewhere. When he told his brother, however, Maurice said that there was no need — they had two chickens and a bit of bacon in the house.

"Maurice," said Ian, "will you look around? There are twenty-five people waiting for lunch."

It was then that grandson Ian made the fitting remark. "Give us five loaves and two fishes," he said, "and I'll show yese all a good trick."

Maurice would have loved that.

Published Works

1905. (?).   *Weekly Freeman story.* (viz "Robbery Under Arms").
1908. Feb.   *Irish Emerald.* "Dick Clinton's Dilemma".
      May.   *Irish Emerald.* "Tearlath O'Daly of Dundareigh".
      July.   *Irish Emerald.* "Eudmon Blake: The Sack of Athenree".
1923. Dec.   *The Dublin Magazine.* Vol 1 No 5. "The Woman Without Mercy".
1924. Aug.   *The Dublin Magazine.* Vol 2 No 1. "The Mission Sermon".
1925. Jan.   *The Dublin Magazine.* Vol 2 No 4. "A Dialogue".
      Dec.   *Chambers Journal. The Key Above the Door.* Dec 1925 – May 1926.
1926. July.   *The Key Above the Door.*
1927. Dec.   *Chambers Journal. While Rivers Run.*
1928.   *While Rivers Run.*
1929. July.   *Chambers Journal. The Small Dark Man.*
      Oct.   *The Small Dark Man.*
1930. June.   *SMT Magazine.* "The Mountain Lands of Badenoch".
      Dec.   *Chambers Journal.* "Over the Border".
1932. Jan.   *Chambers Journal. Blackcock's Feather.*
      July.   *Blackcock's Feather.*
1933. Feb.   *Saturday Evening Post.* "The Quiet Man".
      Aug.   *Chambers Journal.* "The Quiet Man".
               Schools Edition of *Blackcock's Feather.*
1934. May.   *The Road to Nowhere.*
      June.   *Chambers Journal.* "Before Cock Crow".
      Nov.   *Saturday Evening Post.* "Then Came the Captain's Daughter".
1935. May.   *Saturday Evening Post.* "Bad Town Dublin".
      Sept.   *Green Rushes.*
      Dec.   *Saturday Evening Post.* "Thirty Pieces of Copper".
1936. Feb.   *Saturday Evening Post.* "Prudent Dan".
      Apr.   *Saturday Evening Post.* "Thomasheen James and the Canary Bird".
      Aug.   *Saturday Evening Post.* "Thomasheen James and the Running Dog".
1937. Jan.   *Chambers Journal.* "Face of Stone".
               (Also *Elk Magazine*, July 1936).
      Aug.   *And No Quarter.*
      June.   *Saturday Evening Post.* "Thomasheen James and the Absent Minded Professor".
               Cleite Clarcollig.

	Aug.	*Adventure Magazine. And No Quarter.*
	Sep.	*Saturday Evening Post.* "Thomasheen James and the Opprobious Name".
1938.		*Sons of the Swordmaker.*
	Nov.	*Saturday Evening Post.* "Thomasheen James and the Dangerous Age".
1939.	Feb.	*Saturday Evening Post.* "Thomasheen James and the Blind Pension".
	June.	*Saturday Evening Post.* "Thomasheen James and the Birdlover".
	Dec.	*Saturday Evening Post.* "Thomasheen James and the Deep Sea Pilot Cap".
1940.	Jan.	*Saturday Evening Post.* "Thomasheen James Jumps the Budget".
	Jan.	*Saturday Evening Post.* "Ireland in a Warring Europe".
1940.	June.	*Chicago Tribune.* "Thomasheen James and the Gum Drop".
	June.	*Chambers Journal. Son of Apple.*
	July.	*The Hill Is Mine.*
	Oct.	*The Bell*, Vol 1 No 1. "Butcher to the Queen".
	Dec.	*Saturday Evening Post.* "Son of a Tinker".
1941.	May.	*Saturday Evening Post.* "Not My Story".
	Mar.	*Thomasheen James, Man-of-no-Work.*
	Aug.	*The Bell.* "Whiskey".
1943.		*The Spanish Lady.*
	June.	*Chicago Tribune. The Spanish Lady.*
1945.	Feb.	*The Sign.* "The Queen's Dirty Shirts".
	Mar.	*The Man in Brown.*
	July.	*Saturday Evening Post.* "Nine Strings To Your Bow".
1946.		*The Golden Pheasant* (play).
1947.		*Son of Apple.*
1948.		*Castle Gillian.*
	Dec.	*Chambers Journal.* "My Fey Lady".
1950.		*Trouble in the Glen.*
		Scottish Radio broadcast *The Key Above the Door.*
	Oct.	*Chicago Tribune. Trouble in the Glen.*
1951.	Apr.	*Saturday Evening Post.* "The Amateur Doctor".
		Son of a Tinker.
1952.	Apr.	*Chambers Journal.* "The Hoplologist".
		Irish Mist advertisement: "The Secret of the O'Donchu".
1953.	May.	*Saturday Evening Post.* "Come Back My Love".
	Oct.	*Irish Press.* Four articles on whiskey.

Dec.	*Saturday Evening Post.* "Fisherman's Revenge".
	The Honest Fisherman.
1954.	*A Strange Woman's Daughter.*
1956. Jan.	*Chambers Journal.* "Unlimited Liability".
	Danger Under the Moon.
1957.	*The Shannonside Annual.* "A Night in the Highlands".
1961. May.	*Saturday Evening Post.* "Visitor From America".
Oct.	*Saturday Evening Post.* "A Seven Pound Trout".
1963. Mar.	*Fantasy Magazine.* "The Sword of Yung Lo".
1964.	*The Smart Fellow.*

Books published in America by Lipincott / Stokes

Title in the U.S.A.	**Title in the U.K.**
1932. *Blackcock's Feather.*	The same.
1933. *Romantic Adventures*	
(Omnibus).	(*While Rivers Run.*
	(*The Small Dark Man.*
1934. *The Road to Nowhere.*	The same.
1935. *Green Rushes.*	The same.
1936. *Three Roads.* (Omnibus)	(*Blackcock's Feather.*
	(*The Road to Nowhere.*
	(*Green Rushes.*
1937. *The Dark Rose.*	*And No Quarter.*
1938. *Sons of the Swordmaker.*	The same.
1940. *Son of Apple.*	The same.
1940. *The Hill Is Mine.*	The same.
1941. *Thomasheen James.*	*Thomasheen James,*
	Man-of-no-Work.
1943. *The Spanish Lady.*	The same.
1945. *Nine Strings to Your Bow.*	*The Man in Brown.*
1948. *The Damsel Debonair.*	*Castle Gillian.*
1950. *Trouble in the Glen.*	The same.
1951. *Son of a Tinker.*	The same.
1954. *Take Your Choice.*	*The Honest Fisherman.*
1956. *Danger Under the Moon.*	The same.
1964. *Thomasheen James*	
Gets His Hair Cut.	*The Smart Fellow.*

Notes.

1. *Green Rushes,* published 1935. From the story, "Then Came the Captain's Daughter", p 67.
2. From a description amongst the Maurice Walsh papers, prompted by a "Confession" on Irish scenery published in *Irish Travel* by T.C. Murray.
3. The physical characteristics of these different Walsh families – small stature, beaked nose – suggest a blood connection and such limited correspondence as survives indicates that there may in fact have been one. But no detailed family tree now exists (though John and Paddy Walsh once produced one) to support the claim. Maurice Walsh himself was convinced.
4. *While Rivers Run,* 1927. pp 195-6.
5. Ibid. p 328. In fact, the Buchanan story was entitled "Matt: a Story of a Caravan" and it appeared in 1885.
6. *Son of a Tinker,* 1951: from the story "My Fey Lady" at p 167.
7. *The Small Dark Man,* 1929, at pp 161-2.
8. From a letter written in September 1959 to his niece.
9. *The Road to Nowhere,* 1934, at pp 289-90.
10. From a letter written in 1933.
11. From a letter written in April 1950 to his publishers, in connection with the Scottish Radio version of *The Key Above the Door.*
12. From the descriptive piece quoted at 2 above.
13. From a letter to his publishers in May 1950, used as a foreword to J. Marshall Robb's fine book *Scotch Whisky: A Survey.*
14. From the 1926 Report of the General Council.
15. The J. Marshall Robb foreword.
16. Ibid.
17. *The Key Above the Door,* 1925. pp 61-9.
18. "A Night in the Highlands", from *The Shannonside Annual,* 1957.
19. *Son of a Tinker,* 1951, from the story "Butcher to the Queen" which appeared first in 1940.
20. "A Night in the Highlands", as at 18 above.
21. *Son of a Tinker,* from the story "My Fey Lady".
22. P. H. Mooney, reported in *Irisleabhair,* July/August 1934.
23. Letter to Chambers, 28.5.26.
24. *Irisleabhair,* April 1927.
25. The 1926 *Annual Report.*
26. *Irisleabhair,* December 1930.
27. *Irisleabhair,* March, 1934.
28. *Irisleabhair,* July/August 1934.

29.   *The Small Dark Man*, p 131.
30.   From a letter written to his niece in 1933.
31.   In a letter from Brandt and Brandt to Maurice Walsh, dated 2.4.34.
32.   Transcribed from the photograph, amongst the Walsh papers.
33.   *The Hill Is Mine*, 1940, pp 93-4.
34.   *Thirty Pieces of Copper*, published in the *Saturday Evening Post* in December 1935 and collected in *Thomasheen James, Man-of-no-Work*, 1941.
35.   *A Strange Woman's Daughter*, 1954, describing Thady High Gow at p 16.
36.   In a letter from Neil Gunn, in Inverness, in 1934.
37.   Letter to his niece in Scotland, 14.5.41.
38.   "Thomasheen James and the Running Dog", published in the *Saturday Evening Post* in August 1936 and collected in *Thomasheen James, Man-of-no-Work*.
39.   Letter from Neil Gunn, 22.3.40.
40.   From a letter to Chambers, 18.1.37.
41.   Letter from Neil Gunn, 5.2.37.
42.   Letter from Neil Gunn, 23.7.37.
43.   Letter to his niece in Scotland, 21.2.44.
44.   From a letter to Toshon's niece Dodo, after she had written on hearing of her aunt's death, 20.1.41.
45.   Letter to the same niece, 14.5.41.
46.   From the same letter.
47.   Letter to Scotland, 1952.
48.   From a manuscript amongst the Walsh papers.
49.   A letter to Chambers, 30.7.46.
50.   From the manuscript of the screenplay, among the Walsh papers.
51.   In a letter from Neil Gunn, 18.10.54.
52.   Ibid., 3.3.57.
53.   Ibid., September 1957.
54.   *The Hill Is Mine*, pp 137-8.
55.   See, for example, Joseph T. Carroll's *Ireland in the War Years, 1937 - 1945*, published by David and Charles, 1975 and Robert Fisk's *In Time of War*, published by Brandon and Deutsch, 1983.
56.   From a letter to his niece in Scotland, 7.10.41.
57.   Ibid., 30.8.50.
58.   Letter to Scotland, 20.3.57.
59.   A 1916 man – someone who was out in the 1916 Easter Rising.
60.   From a letter to his niece, 14.5.41.
61.   *While Rivers Run*, at p 76.
62.   *The Small Dark Man*, p 161.
63.   *The Key Above the Door*, pp 171-2.

64. Ibid., pp 117-8.
65. *While Rivers Run*, p 260.
66. Ibid., pp 277-8.
67. *The Small Dark Man*, pp 93-4.
68. Letters to his niece, 21.11.44.
69. *The Spanish Lady*, pp 21-2.
70. Ibid., p 203.
71. Ibid., p 51.
72. *The Key Above the Door*, p 54.
73. Ibid., p 71 and p 100.
74. *The Small Dark Man*, p 38.
75. Ibid., p 133-34.
76. *While Rivers Run*, p 195.
77. *The Spanish Lady*, p 77 and pp 184-5.
78. *Trouble in the Glen*, the Song of the Broken Clan, at p 179.
79. *Green Rushes*, pp 69-70.
80. *Blackcock's Feather*, p 105-6.
81. Ibid., p 265.
82. *And No Quarter*, pp 262-3.
83. Letter from Neil M. Gunn, 23.2.37.
84. *Sons of the Swordmaker*, p 9.
85. Letter from Neil M. Gunn, at Braefarm House, Dingwall, 22.3.40.
86. Letter to Chambers, 6.4.40.
87. Letter to his niece in Scotland, 7.10.41.
88. Ibid., 25.8.53.
89. Ibid., 30.5.61.
90. From a poem among the Walsh papers. Some of it appears in *While Rivers Run* at p 238, but Maurice added to it over the years. It was never quite finished.
91. *And No Quarter*, p 168.
92. *The Key Above the Door*, pp185-6.
93. From a letter to his niece, 21.9.43.
94. Ibid., St John's Eve, 1957.
95. *Castle Gillian*, p 128.
96. Letter to his niece, 23.12.24.
97. Ibid., 21.9.43.
98. Ibid., 26.2.59.
99. Ibid., 9.5.60.
100. Ibid., 9.9.59.
101. Ibid., 9.5.60 (although he was wrong about it being common to both sexes).
102. Ibid., 16.11.61.
103. Letter to Andrew Melvin in Scotland, 26.9.63.

Index

ALSO PUBLISHED BY BRANDON

MAN OF THE TRIPLE NAME
by John B. Keane

"This lyrical, most human and highly humourous book." – Benedict Kiely, *The Irish Times*.

"Anybody who enjoys old-style storytelling at its best should reach for *Man of the Triple Name*." – *Irish Post*.

"Highly enjoyable." – *In Dublin*.

"Fascinating." – *Limerick Leader*.

"Hilarious social history." – *Boston Irish News*.

Paperback

OWL SANDWICHES
by John B. Keane

Owl Sandwiches is John B. Keane in light-hearted form; it is John B. Keane the observer of foibles and teller of tales of compellingly dubious veracity; it is John B. Keane, the publican, leaning over the bar with a wink and a nod, and asking, "Did I ever tell you about the time . . .?"

GREEN AND GOLD
The Wrenboys of Dingle
by Steve MacDonogh

"A heartening and very readable account . . . and a valuable historical document . . . liberally sprinkled with excellent photographs." – "Folkland," *RTE Radio 1*.

"It is important in that it charts in some detail one of our great traditions and so, in time, it will itself become part of our folklore. It is written lightly, with that touch of wry Kerry humour which appeals, and is well illustrated." – *Cork Examiner*.

"Amusing, informative and full of local flavour." – *Ireland's Own*.

"Quite an accomplishment . . . Brandon have paid a handsome homage to their place of location." – *Drogheda Independent*.

HERITAGE NOW
Irish Literature in the English Language
by Anthony Cronin

"Anthony Cronin's reading is wide, his insights astonishing, his whole book suggests that we may well be ready for a unitarian approach to the literature of Ireland in English." – *Anthony Burgess*.

"This is a good book to have around. It's at once warm and intelligent in its approach. It has an extremely sensitive feel for the essential qualities of the Irish voice as expressed in literature . . . The verve of the discussion, the vivid connections established, open the topics freshly to us." – *Tom McIntyre*.

"After years of persistent attempts to open up the closed shop of so-called Anglo-Irish literature, Anthony Cronin has flushed it out with an explosive critical device called *Heritage Now*." – *Francis Stuart*.

Brandon Book Publishers Ltd, Dingle, Co. Kerry.